The Un... of Plowing

Unfiltered Memoirs to the American Public
from the Minds of Black Men

VOLUME 1

Shonda Kay White

outskirts
press

Shonda kissing sharecropper (grandfather)

This book is dedicated to Ennis Van Degrate Sr. and his family. Thank you for living your lives in a way that others can aspire to emulate. Your hard work through the years and humble dedication to family and friends speaks volumes to many. I appreciate who you are and the legacy that encourages us all to press onward, looking ahead to that which is Greater.

> "Plow new ground for yourselves, plant righteousness, and reap the blessings that your devotion to me will produce. It is time for you to turn to me, your Lord, and I will come and pour out blessings upon you." (Hosea 10:12)

Your Granddaughter

This book is also dedicated to the four men who helped make this project possible by sharing the deepest parts of their hearts and minds for the very first time. I am forever grateful for their trust in me to deliver their words of wisdom and raw experiences to the American public. Thank you!

SKW

What Readers are Saying ......

"*The Understatement of Plowing* captured my attention from the start. Black and white males of all ages would certainly benefit from these memoirs by learning history through the eyes of American black men who have endured the process of paving the way in hopes of securing a better future for younger generations to come."

—Lenoy Jones Sr., Former NFL Player

"Insightful ... genuine ... pertinent ... hopeful ... Captures how far each generation has come in improving opportunity for black men; and yet how far is still to go. By asking the same questions of four generations of black men, Shonda White captures the common desire of each for fair opportunities and to be valued for the person they are beneath their skin."

—Hylie Voss, Managing Director of
Sugarbush Valley, LLC,
Athens, Ohio

Table of Contents

Introduction i

Part 1

1. The Mourner's Bench 3
2. Poisoned Cotton 22
3. Eight-Day Pneumonia 31

Part 2

4. Born Off the Farm..47
5. An Unfair Deal 57

Part 3

6. A Cause for Justice 73
7. Perceptions...86

Part 4

8. Millennial Memoirs 103
9. Waiting for Change.......................................109

Author's Conclusion 117

Introduction

IN JUNE OF 2019, I asked a series of thought-provoking questions to four black men from different walks of life, comprised of four generations and a completion of 249 years. The interviews were conducted separately within four days. The answers I received as the interviewer are different responses, yet similar connotations that bring forth the expressions of heartfelt needs, desires, experiences, and convictions. They know their own opinions are just that ... THEIR OWN ... and they are okay with that. They formed their opinions patiently and observantly as life lessons from secondhand books rationed in their direction were disguised as fair offerings. These are perspectives gathered collectively as they journey in a society that has not always been kind to them. But some make a claim to fame that it is what it is, and things are seemingly better than what they used to be. "Where is the gratitude? You have come a long way, be satisfied. Stand down and hold your face against the sand. No need to bury it any longer, just keep it down without being bothersome and we will try not to trip over you. Do not think more highly of yourselves than you ought to think. Here is your place, stay in it. If you attempt to cross that boundary, you will be more than reprimanded." A second chance or clean slate is almost invisible against the smallest mistakes. And we cannot forget about the common labels attached to already tainted portfolios that keep them herded in fine lines of discouragement, whether through psychological methods or mere prejudgments. Either way, labeling has always been an enemy of the black man. And he has yet to overcome the threat of character assassination and unexplained preconceived notions initially based on the color of his skin. His actions are under a microscope and his intents are under constant scrutiny, from the tone of his voice to the gestures of his body language. How can he win? Which way is the acceptable way? If he cannot mirror his counterparts, he is in trouble. So, this is the way of the world in most cases for the black man. And although he is in continual pursuit of shattering misconceptions and restoring his identity, his case is still rugged, torn, aged, and in need of repair. A repair that can begin with an attentive ear and a grasp of understanding, if only the slightest. And with the slightest understanding, a level of regard and an ounce of respect is mustered because what you hear is brokenness and division (damaged, pulled apart, and/or separated). Divided in nature, self, and society. The four men spoke not knowing that they deeply wanted to be heard, only answering the questions as honestly as their souls would allow. Their voices were not loud or disruptive, and they did not need to flash statements of physical gestures, or wave banners protesting for freedom and equality. The simple fact that someone asked made all the difference in the world. Because if someone asked, it meant they cared, if only in the least diminutive measure. For a moment, they are known and not waiting to be judged. Their lives are not affected or interrupted by the decisions and plans of others. What if white privilege took a back seat for a moment, allowing room for others? Or, what if everyone shared the exact same privileges? Well, I guess it would no longer be a privilege, now would it? It would then be considered FAIR.

It is difficult to associate with or appreciate what we do not understand. But to extend support and encouragement would surely break down walls that separate us as people. There have been many trials, heartaches, miscommunications, misunderstandings, misconceptions, preconceived notions, and an ample amount of disunity that has overshadowed our society far too long. Have you ever asked yourself, "I wish I knew more about him?" Or "I wish I knew how to relate to him, be his friend and simply find some common ground with him?"

If these thoughts have never entered your mind, then you may need to check your heart as to where you stand concerning life and its complicated realities of relationships and decency towards fellow men.

I was floored by the voices that I heard and the answers that were spoken. I heard them with a sense that was far beyond my physical ears to hear and a mind to quickly process. I listened and received from the core of my being because that is what was touched: the core of my being. Each man experiencing a battle to remain unbroken and to sustain his original identity as given to him by God, not man.

Their words moved me and encouraged me to be a better person, not for myself but for God and others. Their experiences raised an awareness that stimulated the idea of never settling for less than God's best and living peaceably with all men, never discounting them, no matter their race, culture, social or economic status.

Many are disturbed and dumbfounded by a system that has compromised its moral compass on the value of life. Our society is on the brink of destroying itself all while trying to eliminate those that help make it great. As a thriving nation, America has been through a lot, but the wicked nature of division continues to prevail, and we cannot believe that God is pleased with that. Why bring God into this? Because He is the creator of the universe and of all mankind. His intentions were never for us to be divided, but to walk together in unison.

I hope the words of these four men will be received with the same eye-opening perspective that I encountered. If it touches you at the core of your being, then there is hope, and hope does not disappoint. If it nudges you like a soft tap from behind and you acknowledge it enough to turn around, then there is a slow awakening taking place in your heart and hope lies just around the corner. To think that we live in a fair and just society that is getting better and changing with time means absolutely nothing if hearts remain the same. This has been proven for decades. The only one that can truly testify that racial unity is on the rise is the one that has been oppressed, not his oppressor. The fact that the oppressor believes that he has the right to make that determination says it all: "Things are not on the rise as we would hope." The biggest obstacles that have slowed down transformation in our country are matters of the heart. A heart that harbors hatred, ignorance, fear, manipulation, jealousy, and unforgiveness is disturbed and misguided. This type of heart can be inside any race of people.

As you read their words, sit back and absorb every line. Grasp what is being said like your life depends on it (well ... maybe not your life, but the life of another) and take note of how it feels to be A Black Man. You will never know until you choose to know. And when you truly know, there is a sensible awareness that allows healthy empathy.

Nothing really is fair game in an unfair world that subtly demands that you "FIT" the mold they have created for you or quietly step aside. Plowing through stubborn ground and waiting for the ultimate harvest of true equality can seem tiresome and full of defeat. But four generations share their stories of never giving up in a land that has promised them the fruit of liberty and justice for all.

PART 1

CHAPTER 1

The Mourner's Bench

He sat in a big comfy chair at the gracious old age of ninety-six wearing what I have known him to wear most of his life: a white collared shirt with denim blue overalls that carried pens in the front slip pocket, brown industrial socks, and standard black work shoes. It was the relaxing attire of familiarity. His glasses sat upright on his dark brown face as the words that he spoke left his mouth with slurs of excitement, reminiscing of what used to be. His back curved slightly as he leaned forward to make sure I was attentive to what he had to say. But there was no need—I was captivated from the start. A man born in 1922 with a memory and articulation that far exceeded many young people of today. His mind was sharp and on point, unlike the ever-changing short gray hair that slightly dusted the top of his head. At times, he rubbed his legs just below his knees, like it was a comfort of some sort. Other times he held one hand with the other, fidgeting each of the rough, wrinkled members that displayed the mirror of extreme hard work through the years. He is a hero in his own right—seeing, hearing, and experiencing ninety-six years of worldly mundane, hardly forgetting any of it, although at times he would like to.

But his strength, perseverance, and self-dignity outweighed all obstacles that have ever stood before him.

Not once was there any hesitation to answer the questions that I asked him. The eagerness in his voice was like a shout from a mountaintop, yet the sound that came from his mouth was more than pleasant; it soothed my listening ears. His gestures were calm and peaceful without regret, willingly open to a dialogue of the unspeakable. Someone asked and he was compelled to oblige. I knew that my interview with him would be lengthy. It gives part of a faulty foundation laid somewhere between 1865 (when slavery was abolished) and 1922 (his introduction into the so-called free nation). It was imperative to capture many of his experiences to set the tone for the other three interviews placed in different generations.

I sat across from him with my phone in hand reading the first question from my Notebook app, explaining to him that the questions were stored on the small device. Of course, he thought it was fascinating how today's phones could be used for more than just talking. But he was ready and so the interview began …

"How did you feel as a child in the early 1920s and '30s being black? What were the differences you noticed?"

He leaned forward and stared in my direction, looking over the rims of his thick glasses and clearing his throat. I could tell that he was contemplating his answers as he began rubbing his knees with wrinkled hands that could tell a few stories of their own.

"I'm trying to think. Um, black people stayed mostly to themselves in my day, you know. They did not mix with white folks. Among the black people, we had parties and suppers, and we felt good because back in those days, blacks did not worry too much about being segregated. Look like to me they were satisfied. All that black people worried about in the 1920s and '30s was living and getting something to eat." (He snickers as if he had made a joke.)

Then he takes more of a serious demeanor and grabs both knees, rubbing them vigorously, looking down at the floor as though it spoke to him, giving him answers. I knew that he was thinking, traveling back to his past when things were simpler, but still complicated to say the least. When Ennis Degrate Sr. was born in 1922, it had only been fifty-seven years since slavery had been abolished. It passed the Senate on April 8, 1864 and passed the House on January 31, 1865. It was not until June 19, 1865 that slavery was abolished in the great state of Texas.

"Um ... 1930, let me see. In 1930 Bub was born (his little brother). That was when the water in the Brazos River came all the way up to where Mt. Olive Church is now, where the Red River was before they built Putney Lake. All that flooded. That Red River came up and we had to come out and get to the top of the hill in Downsville (small town outside of Waco, Texas). That is where we stayed. I remember we had cotton about as high as this (he gestures with his hands, showing us the height of about 3 feet). Water got over it. When it was ready to pick, we had to go out there and pick it. It was mud all over the bulbs. We pulled the mud off the cotton when it was dry and carried it to the gin.

We sold it cheap cause of the mud, but we got rid of it."

"How old were you?" I asked in curiosity, knowing that he must have been quite young in the '30s.

"I was eight years old."

"You picked cotton at eight years old?"

"Yeah ..." he said proudly with a high-pitched voice. "I was picking cotton at eight years old and chopping and going on at eight."

"Did you get paid?"

"Huh?"

"Did you get paid?"

"Fifty cents a day. All day, from sunup to sundown."

His voice became high pitched again as the memories surfaced in his mind. His wife echoes in the background that she had done the same thing (picked cotton).

"Until sundown. Fifty cents a day," she echoed.

"You didn't go by a clock either, you went by your shadow," she added.

"Your shadow? So, if you could not see your shadow on the ground, you could go home?"

Ennis nodded his head and continued with his story, looking at his wife as though she was interrupting his interview time. So, he continued …

"You didn't sit at the house either. You picked cotton with a tow-sack and they hung them on the children too. We had smaller sacks. But the older folks had big sacks. We had the tow-sacks and had to pull them sacks at eight years old, then empty them in a pound sack. It wasn't big enough to weigh itself."

"So, the money that you made was used to help your family?" I asked.

"Yeah, the money we made, we lived out of it. We were share-croppers. My daddy was a sharecropper and uh … we didn't see money 'til we got through and got all the cotton out of the fields and the Boss Man sold it. No, we did not see no money. And then if we owed the Boss Man …" "Owed the Boss Man? So, you weren't making fifty cents a day?"

"Huh?"

"Cause, you said you were making fifty cents a day, but you didn't see any money."

"That is because I am talking about picking cotton. Chopping is when they pay you by the day. They did not pay you by the hour. They would not let you work by no hour. You worked by the day, from sunup to sundown. Then you got one set amount at the end of the day."

(Chopping equaled end of the day payment. Picking equaled no payment until the "Boss Man" sold the cotton.)

"Yeah, and they wouldn't let you go inside to get water either. They would bring it to you in the fields."

(They had a water boy. It will be explained further in the interview.)

"And if you had to help somebody else, and they hired you, a lot of times the Boss Man would not give you any money. He would give you a piece of paper, like a receipt. Then you went to the store and you bought your groceries with the receipt. You did not get any money."

"Wow ... So, was that still like slavery?"

"Yeah, it was. And you could not go to no bank either. We didn't ever go to a bank."

"So, you did everything based on a piece of paper given to you by the Boss Man?"

"Yeah, just like you get a receipt when you buy something. That is the way it was. You gave the man at the store the receipt or slip of paper and he would sell you groceries."

"Let me see if I am getting this straight. So ... if you worked for a week, that is $2.50? Or did you work seven days in a week?"

"If you were chopping, you could get up to $1.00 a day, depends. And if you worked until dinner on Saturdays, you would get $5.50, depends."

"Was that good money back then?"

"Yeah. My daddy and all them were plowing, you know ... the fields, and they got a dollar a day. And when it came to Saturdays, it was $5.50. Then Saturday evenings you could go and get your groceries. Two or three families would get in a wagon and go to the grocery store. It would take them half a day to go to the store and come back home."

"What store were you going to? Were you going to the white man's store or a black man's store?" "The white man's store. You know where 3rd Street is in Waco?"

"Yes."

"After you pass Mt. Olive Church, coming down to Asa, that is where we went to the store. They sold us shoes and overalls, like these." He looks down at his overalls.

"Is that why you still wear overalls?"

He smiles and then his smile quickly turns to a chuckle. We laughed at the fact that he was still wearing them after all these years (we, as in myself, the cameraman, and Ennis' wife).

"So how many children in your family worked in the fields? Because if you have seven kids working in the fields at fifty cents a day, that's good."

"Yeah, if they were big enough to work, they could get fifty cents. And like I pulled corn for $1.50 per wagon load and then unloaded it." "How long did it take to get a wagon load?"

"We pulled about two loads a day. It would be two of us. That is $3.00. When you got it full, you had to carry it and scoop it out, then unload it and throw it up in the barn. And like if you wanted water, you could not go get any, they sent water boys to go around to wherever you were. They would tote water all day long in buckets. They had a fifty-pound barrel on a two-wheeled cart and a mule pulled it. The water boy would go to the barrel and fill a bucket up with water and come around and give it to each person in the field. And sometimes I would be at the end of a row in the field." (Meaning if you were at the end of a row, it would be awhile before you would receive a bit of water.)

He was more than expressive with his gestures describing the cart that carried their water. I could imagine a smoking hot Texas day. No doubt, it was brutal working conditions. I am sure the heat was exasperating as each one leaked of salty liquid from their pores. But for the time, this was their lot in life. It is what they did, and all that they knew. They began their chores at home first before the sun came up and then went to work the farms and crops of others at daybreak until they could not see their shadows any longer.

"So ... some differences were, you were paid in paper (a receipt) instead of cash, and you worked all day for a small amount of money? But for you as a black man in the '20s and '30s, this was considered good money?"

"Yes, because you could buy a bottle of soda for a nickel and you could get a hamburger for twenty-five cents. You could also get a ring of bologna for a dime. They would give you the crackers for free."

"Free crackers? Man, things have changed." We laughed again.

"What were the staple conversations of black men in the 1930s and '40s?" He scratched his head a bit before answering.

"Well, we talked about fishing and hunting, because that is what we knew a lot about. A few of them talked about church. When I was young, they had a bench at the church. They called it the Mourner's Bench. This was a bench meant for all the sinners. They would send all the young boys outside to get their religion. We would be out by the cotton fields and the woods. I remember one time we were in the woods and a Mexican boy came along. We were all scattered out, you know, somewhere laying on our faces praying. It would be a boy over here and a boy over there. That Mexican did not know what we were doing. He said, 'Potna, Potna ("Partner, Partner" was a friendly name used by some male Hispanics to other males), what's the matter?'

"I did not say a word, so... he just stood there and looked for a while, then walked away. (He laughed as he remembered his childhood.) He probably thought that we were crazy."

"When we went into the church, we sat on the Mourner's Bench as the Pastor preached. If they asked us about our religion and we did not get it right, we had to continue sitting on the Mourner's Bench until we got it right. Some never did get it right. I got it right at the age of seventeen. I could finally join the church."

Wow, you could not be a part of the church until you found your religion. That was interesting to me. But I continued my probing ...

"Did you talk about women?" He leaned over to pull up his socks.

"A few of them talked about women, but it was different back then. A whole lot different. A black woman had to make her dresses out of flour sacks." He frowned as if to say, that was not attractive at all.

"We bought flour fifty pounds at a time. You could not get no ten pounds' sack of flour. They didn't have that."

Then at his pause, his wife added, "And they didn't allow you to have but two pairs of shoes a year." "How many?"

"Just two pairs. They had flour-sack dresses, and women did not hardly go to the store. The men went. Back then, a woman could not hardly buy anything. You are talking about going somewhere to get something? A woman couldn't go any-where and buy anything."

Of course, I was still dumbfounded at the fact that they were only allowed two pairs of shoes a year.

"How did that make you feel?" I asked.

He humbly lifted his head and replied, "We were grateful."

My concept of it all was inconceivable. Everything being rationed to you as though you were property under a strict dictatorship. For me it seemed no different than a Nazi take-over. It was all happening around the same time (1939 was when the Nazis took over Poland).

"Oh yeah. I remember one time I had a play at school, and I needed some new pants to wear. I told my papa about it and he said, 'I tell you what, go to the Boss Man and ask him. See if he can get you a pair of pants.'

"I got up early the next morning and walked to see Boss Man. I went to his back door because you could not go through the front door if you were black. I went to the back door through the kitchen.

"I said, 'Mr. Rice, Papa told me to come out here and ask you if I could get a pair of pants and a pair of shoes for school.' He sat there for a while and did not say anything.

"Then he said, 'You go back there and tell Thomas and Charlie (my papa and my uncle; he never did call one name without the other) they need to be more careful down there. And I tell you what, boy, you go on over there to the store and wait there.'

"So, I rushed out and went to the store and waited. Mr. Rice (Boss Man) came directly. He walked around there. 'What did you say you want, boy?'

"I said, 'I want some shoes and pants for school.'

"Then he demanded that the store man give them to me. 'Walter, let this here boy have a pair of shoes and some pants.'

"Um… it was easier than I thought. Scratching my head, I added, 'I need two pairs of pants.'

"Boss Man looked confused. 'What you gonna do with two pair, boy?'

"'One is for my brother. We both got to have them.' "'Walter, let this boy have a piece of paper.' "I had to write down what I wanted.

"I gave it to Mr. Rice (Boss Man) and he looked over it, then gave it to Walter, the man who ran the store. 'Let this boy have what's on the paper. And boy, you go back and tell Thomas and Charlie they need to be more careful down there.'

(As the interviewer, I was still not sure what that meant. It may have been a reference to the fact that Thomas and Charlie had been treading dangerous waters and needed to be reminded to stay in their place.)

"I walked back home, and my papa was so surprised to see that I had the pants and shoes. He did not think that I had the nerve to go and ask the Boss Man.

"I got me two pairs of pants, a shirt, and a pair of shoes. Papa did not know what to say.

"My brother and I later went to the school and said our speeches. Yeah, that was some time back then."

We continued with more questions as the moment allowed. With each answer, our curiosity was enticed to hear more of this man's history.

THE MOURNER'S BENCH: You are ready to accept Christ when we say that you are ready? There are question marks all over that concept. Oh, and you can get a pair of shoes and pants when we say that you can? Even bigger question marks. You had to remain in a sad needy state until someone else believed that you were worthy of receiving, whether it was for your salvation that was freely given or for your right to get a much-needed pair of pants in the sweet land of liberty. Mind you, this was in the late 1920s and early 1930s. Slavery officially ended in Texas on June 19, 1865, which was months later after it was abolished on January 31, 1865. The final issue of Emancipation Proclamation was set by President Lincoln on January 1, 1863. Slave owners kept the news from their slaves for two years.

(According to Dictionary.com, *Mourner's Bench* was a bench or seat at the front of the church or room, set apart for mourners or penitent sinners seeking salvation. Also, according to Wikipedia, the Mourner's Bench, also known as the mercy eat or anxious bench in the Methodist and other evangelical Christian churches is a bench located in the front of the chancel.

The practice was instituted by John Wesley, founder of the Methodist Church.

"How did you make it through the Texas heat in the summertime without air-conditioning?" He smiled. "We slept on the porch. We did not have any fans, not even electricity. We did not have lights. We burnt lamps (coal oil lamps). We slept on the porch where mosquitoes nearly ate us up. We would build trash fires in the yard and put old rags and stuff in it so that the smoke would keep the mosquitoes away. Sometimes we just laid there in the smoke. It was too hot to stay in the house all the time. It was cooler to be outside. I slept on the porch a many of nights. Sometimes I would sleep in the cornfields, and no one would bother me either."

"What was it like for a white family in those times?"

"Oh, some of them would sleep on their porches too. But they had screened-in porches." He snickered and went right into another story that was prompted by his memory.

"I remember when Papa would get drunk as a young man. One evening, he was riding a horse on his way home. Before he made it home, he got to these white folks' house that was not that far from us, and he thought that he was at home. He got off his horse, walked up to their house, and passed them as they were sitting on the porch looking right at him. He opened their front door and went directly into their house and got into their bed." He could hardly finish speaking because he was laughing extremely hard as he told the story. We were laughing as well.

"I'm surprised he didn't get into serious trouble."

"Well, they knew him, so they just went in behind him and got him up and brought him home." He continued ...

"Then there was another time that Papa got drunk and he passed out in the freezing cold weather outside. It was rainy and muddy. The rain was frozen solid like ice. Papa fell in front of Ms. Fannie and Jim Hicks' house. They lived up the road from us. He was coming home with some whiskey in a bucket. And he got to drinking out of the bucket on his way home and became drunk. He passed out on the cold ground and froze. He was stiff when they brought him to the house." (He laughed even more as his thoughts displayed a picture in his mind.)

"You see, Ms. Fannie was going out to their outhouse that evening (we did not have no indoor toilets back then) and she heard a noise down the road. She and Mr. Jim went to see what it was. Well ... it was Papa down there, so they hooked up the wagon, put him on the back of it, and brought him home. I remember we had a fireplace, so they built a big fire then drug him in and laid him down in front of it. They used a spoon to scoop out the mud that was frozen to his eyelids. He finally came through, waking up and looking around at all of us. It was kind of funny. Do you know that he never got sick from that? He lived to be 94 years old."

He said that with pride in his voice.

"I have known you for years and have never known you to drink anything."

"No, I don't drink anything but water. I am not like my papa was. I never did drink anything. The only thing I did when I was young was smoked. I smoked a little, but I didn't drink."

"Did you ever taste it or try it?"

"Well, I got with a bunch of guys one time and they were all drinking and asked me to take a drink. I took a swallow or two and it made me sick. I was a grown man then. I never drank again after that. I do not drink beer. I do not drink wine. I do not drink whiskey. I never drink. I did smoke for about fifteen or twenty years. Then it got to where I could not breathe sometimes. I could not make it to the job that I walked to every day. I did not have a car at the time, so I usually walked everywhere. It was to the point that I could not make it without stopping to rest and had to walk miles and miles to get to work. That is the reason I had to stop smoking." "What did you do when it was raining?"

"I walked in the rain. It did not matter what the weather was like. If it was work, I had to go."

"Are you content with the way society has treated black men?"

"Uh … I am somewhat content with it because back in those days what they did was kept you living." (*Content* was a word with a stronger meaning back then. To him, *content* meant he did not have a choice but to be satisfied, and that was simply because he was alive. I am sure that he heard plenty of stories from his father and others about the "Waco Horror" that happened seven years before his birth. It was the horrific 1916 lynching of a seventeen-year old disabled black man who was a farmhand accused of murdering a white woman. He was dragged, beaten, stabbed, castrated, and then lynched near Waco's city hall in front of 10,000 or more spectators who celebrated.)

"But they would always get the benefit of keeping you alive. They needed you to work their farms and their fields. They kept you living with a little bit of food, and a place to stay on their farms. Back then I had to be content because of the circumstances. Today I am content because it is better than what it used to be.

"We did what we had to do to hustle. That is all we knew. I do not mean *hustle* in a bad way. I mean, we had to work things out the best we could. And you had better not steal anything to feed your family. I once knew a young black man who was sentenced to one year in jail for stealing a chicken to feed his family." "Really?"

"Yeah, they would put a black man in jail real quick back in those days. That is why it was sometimes best to just keep to yourself so that you would not run into trouble.

"I sat in houses where you could see chickens walking under the house from the inside. When I was a little boy, like nine or ten years old, I tried to catch a rooster by sticking my hands down through the cracks in the floor and grabbing its tail." He leans over to demonstrate his rooster-hunting skills to us as we laughed.

"It doesn't sound logical, but it's true."

"So, you are content because they kept you alive, although it was for their benefit?"

"Yeah, and another thing. If you were considered bad, you could not get a job on any other farm. They would alert one another (white folks). If you wanted to move from one man's farm to another, they would ask who you were living with. If you were a good person, then you would not have no trouble, and you would make it. But if you did something they did not like, you would not get any work to take care of your family.

"I remember following my brother on the way to school one day. We went through the woods where trees had been cut down. The stumps were still high. One of the stumps tripped me and the other one caught my knee. I did not go to a doctor. My mamma put soot from the fireplace on my knee. They used old made-up stuff. That is the way that it healed. We hardly ever went to a doctor back then. We could not. You had to get permission from the Boss Man before you could see a doctor.

"So ... just recently, I went to the doctor for a checkup and she was looking at my knee and noticed the scar. I told her what happened when I was a boy and that it bothers me sometimes.

"The nurse was shocked. It had been nearly ninety years since it happened. I guess I broke something that really did not heal completely. I just remember that at seven years old I couldn't walk on it for about a month."

"How many miles was it for you to walk to school?"

"About four miles."

"You walked four miles every day to get to school?"

"Yeah, four miles there and four miles back home."

"What did you do when it rained?"

"I walked. I had to cross a creek. When the creek was up, we had to use a foot log to get across. It was a big log too. You could not walk it because if you did, you could flip over. You had to crawl on it to get across."

(In other words, you did what you had to do to make it. You weathered the storms and rain without complaint, and you maneuvered over obstacles that stood in your way. There was no time for "MOURNING.")

"The truth about black history is that the truth is so much more complex than anything you can make up." —Henry Louis Gates

CHAPTER 2

Poisoned Cotton

"You raised how many children?"

"Eight."

"And you were never on welfare or used any type of government assistance?"

(According to the Constitutional Rights Foundation cfr-usa. org, in 1935, a national welfare system had been established for the first time in American history.)

"Never. And you can ask any of my children if they were ever hungry. We had everything that we needed. I had hogs. I had cows. I had chickens. I had turkeys. I had guineas. And on top of all that, I hunted. I would bring back rabbit and ..."

"Wait, you have to be a pretty good shot to shoot a rabbit."

"We not only shot rabbits, we killed them with rocks too."

"Rocks?"

"Yeah, we killed rabbits a many of days with rocks and sticks. The boys (his sons) could throw like I do not know what! If they got the rabbit hemmed up, they could catch it." He said that with more excitement in his voice.

"It was much better once I became an adult. When I was a child, we never even thought about eating steak for your supper. The only cow that my papa had was used for milk. We could not kill it for beef. In fact, my mamma used to trade that cow's milk for eggs.

"The Mexicans that lived near us had plenty of chicken eggs, but they needed milk. And that is when the trading began."

"Are you proud of all your children and the way that they turned out?"

"Oh yeah, I am proud of all my children and I love them all. I do not have one that I do not love. I would give my life for either of them. I raised a good bunch of kids. I tell you what, you don't want to mess with any of my kids if you don't want to get the Old Man stirred up."

"Even Ennis Junior (his eldest son)?"

"Yeah, even Junior. Now, I thought that Kenneth (youngest son) would give me trouble, and he did for a while, but he straightened up. And that goes to show you that if you raise a child a certain way in a family, he may stray off for a while, but he will come back to his learning. Kenneth is doing just as good as the rest of them now. My biggest backers when they were young were Jeanette, Betty, and Junior.

They helped a lot around the house. Doris mostly babysat. That is what she liked to do."

"What about Edward Charles (next to the youngest)?"

"Edward Charles has always been a champion since he came into the world. When he was little, he would get up early on Sunday mornings and go down to the club (Juke Joint) to hunt for money (money left over from those who drank too much to realize that they may have dropped coins or cash). Edward Charles would come back with a pocket full of coins. He was no bigger than that (he shows us by measuring about three or four feet high with his hand just to show how tall Edward was). Yeah, I raised a good family. The best thing about it, I never had any trouble out of them. You know, like fighting or hitting. And I never had to whoop them. Well, I did whoop Junior and Red (Robert, the middle son) one time about a cat."
"A cat?"

"Yeah, I had this old tom cat one time. And one morning my wife and I were getting ready to go into town and I told Junior and Red (Robert) to watch that old cat and to make sure that he did not scratch the baby (Edward Charles as an infant). When we came back home, I walked in the kitchen and those boys had that cat tied up to the table (he burst out with laughter and a high-pitched voice, barely spitting out his words). They had his legs tied so tight that the cat did not have any circulation, which caused it to swell. That poor cat. I tore those boys up (a very good spanking). They said, 'Well Daddy, you told us not to let that cat scratch the baby. We did what you told us to do.'

"That is the only time I remember whooping them. Then I had my youngest girl, Gloria Jean. She was a good girl too. All eight of them were good, four boys and four girls." (In loving memory of Red.)

"Have you ever been made to feel inferior to another race or culture?"

"Well, I always thought I was just as good as anybody else. That is just the way that I felt at the time. But I have been made to feel inferior to the white race to some degree. That is the way things were back then. They were always trying to make you feel less than what you were to keep control of you. One time I was working on a job in Waco and I was up in the ceiling of a building. It had these pipes running through it. Sawdust would go through the pipes. I was the one who was hired to unstop the pipes. A young white foreman came in and started hollering at me. Now, that is one thing that I cannot stand. If you want to make me mad quick, holler at me.

You can say the same words to me in a low tone, but do not holler at me. I do not like that.

"So, this foreman said, 'Hey! Hey! What you are doing up there?!'

"Well, I was supposed to be up there. This guy was a young one. He was a little boss man. I came down off that pipe and got a two-by-four (in case he needed to protect himself). There were other black folks standing around watching this little boss man holler at me. I noticed this other black guy that I grew up with me. He was watching too. When I got down from that ceiling, do you know that I never stop walking? I walked out of that building and the little boss man continued yelling at me and saying all kinds of things. And then he started following me. I walked straight to my car, and the other black guy I knew was right behind me in case he needed to help me out. He said that if that little boss man tried to jump on me, he was going to put something on him."

"So, you had some help?"

"Yeah, but I was just going to my car. I left the job that day and never went back. It was a good job too, but he kept hollering at me with so much disrespect. I just could not stand it. See, I knew what he was doing so I had to get away from there. I just walked away."

(Remember to remove yourself from a hostile and toxic environment where you are the target. Nothing good can come from it. It is like poison and your perpetrators will not relent until you are gone or better yet, destroyed. It is important to recognize when you are being provoked.)

"How long did you live on the Boss Man's farm back in the day?"

"Only two of my kids were born on a white man's farm. I married in 1941 to Eula Evans. Our oldest child Jeanette was born in 1941. Our second child, Betty, was born in 1944, and Junior was born in 1946. Junior was not born on no white man's farm. Junior was the first child of mine born on my daddy-in-law's place, the Evans' farm." "Where was the Evans' farm located?"

"Right there down from where we now have the family reunions. That was the Evans' farm. They had 75 acres, and no one really wanted to work it. So, when my mother-in-law passed away, me and my family moved away from the Boss Man's farm and in with my daddy-in-law to help him. My wife (his daughter) would cook and clean for him and I worked the farm. We lived with him for fifteen or sixteen years. He had some old horses that I worked. The blood weeds around that place were nearly taller than the house. I drugged them down with a plow and put stuff in its place. I kept doing that until the land was the way it was supposed to be. And my papa gave me a heifer when I was first married. I kept that old cow for a long time. She birthed fourteen calves before she died and every one of them were heifers, except for one. I built from that. My daddy-in-law had some cows, so he let me have what he had. I bought mules and worked the land. I made pretty good money in the 1950s. One morning this white guy that I had been doing some work for came over. I was just sitting there milking a cow and here he comes with a nice big tractor on his truck. I was surprised because I had never said nothing to him about a tractor. He was running this John Deere place in Marlin, Texas. He come up and said, 'Ennis, I brought you this tractor.'

"So, I asked, 'What am I going to do with a tractor?'

"'Well, you need to get rid of those old mules and start farming like other folks.'

"So, I told him, 'I ain't got no money to buy it.' "Then he said, 'Well, you don't need no money.'" "So ... he gave you a tractor?" I asked.

"No, I had to pay for it, but I didn't have to pay anything down. I just made payments on it. I turned around and sold all that I had accumulated. I had a barn full of corn and about 400 bales of hay. I sold all that to black people who were trying to farm. White folks did not buy any, but black folks did. When I was done, I had quite a pile of money. I was the first black man in this area to have my own John Deere tractor. I took that tractor and worked all the land around there. Some years later, I decided to buy me a bigger tractor. (Sometimes, all it takes is a little jump start from someone to help you move forward. Not a handout, but a jump start. Every man can benefit from one.)

"I worked and rented land between Asa and Highway 77. It was about 180 so acres." "You rented land?"

"Yeah, I ran that whole farm. I had that and my boys worked too. At that time, I was working all that land and driving a school bus too. I believe that was the year that I got sick. It was in the 1950s. I got poisoned and had to go into the hospital. Junior was about seven years old. I remember they would not let him in the hospital to see me and he was upset about that. He was too small. My mamma brought him around to the windows of my hospital room. I was on the bottom floor. She let him look in the window at me as I lay in the bed. When he crawled up to the window, I talked to him. What happened was, I had been working for another white guy, helping him all day, and I was tired and hungry. I come in that evening and my wife had cooked me some okra, cabbage, and greens. Boy, I was hungry. I ate all the food that night and felt sick to my stomach right after. But what we later realized is that it was not all the food that made me feel bad. It was something else.

"I had been picking what we called 'Poisoned Cotton' (cotton already sprayed with methyl parathion: a pesticide). While picking the cotton, I had on cloth gloves that had gotten wet. This caused the poison to get in the gloves and then on my hands and into my bloodstream. I remember going to the store one day and this white guy that I knew noticed that I did not look right. He said, 'Hey Ennis, what's wrong with you?' I said, 'I don't know.' He said, 'Boy, you better get out of here and go to the doctor. Ain't you looked down at yourself? Your stomach is swollen.'

"My stomach was way out there. I took him at his word and went to the doctor. They carried me to Dr. Smalls there in East Waco. First, they said that it was my kidneys, then they figured out that it was the poison from the cotton. I stayed in the hospital for fourteen days. They washed me out thoroughly. They kept flushing my intestines until I got right. My stomach has not been the same since. I have been bothered with my stomach since the 1950s."

"That was back when there was a lot of racial tension, right?"

"Yeah, but we all just kept to ourselves pretty much. That's what we always did so we would not have trouble."

(Just like the cotton, if you come in close contact with it at the wrong time, it could hurt you.)

"If there is no struggle, there is no progress." —Frederick Douglas

CHAPTER 3

Eight-Day Pneumonia

"The late 1920s and early '30s was a lot different than the '50s. In the 1950s we could take ourselves to the doctor without permission, but in the '20s and '30s we still needed permission from the Boss Man. I remember being a small boy and wanting to go to school one morning. I woke up early just before daylight and it was foggy and raining outside. Papa told me, 'Son, if you finish planting them rows of corn, you can go to school when you're done.'

"So, I got out there in the fog and misting rain and ran the mule. I was not walking him. I ran him, making him kind of trot, you know. I had to hurry up and get through so that I could go to school. "When I finally got to school that morning, I had not been there an hour before I realized I was sick. I was not feeling good at all. The teacher asked another boy in my class to walk me home. I could not walk alone. As we were walking four miles to my house, the rain continued to fall. When we got to a barbed-wire fence, the boy tried to get me through the fence, and the wire cut me right here (he points to his left hip). It hurt very badly. When I got home, Papa could not call no doctor. He had to go find the Boss Man, which was about six miles on a mule, so that he could get permission for a doctor.

"While I waited, my mamma and Miss Marie were rubbing me with ointment and all kinds of stuff. They were doctoring on me for hours. Later that day, the doctor showed up. He looked me over and told my parents that I had the Eight-Day Pneumonia and there was nothing that they could do but wait. If I made it eight days and the fever broke, then I would live. If not, I would die. Well, I made it eight days and the fever broke, but I could not go back to school for a long time. I stayed sickly for a while."

"So, according to what I am hearing you say today, there were two times that you could have died. Once when you had the Eight-Day Pneumonia as a child, and the other time as an adult when your intestines were swollen and infected by

Poisoned Cotton? And all this took place as you were working on the Boss Man's farm?"

"Yeah."

"So, let me ask you something; none of us are going to live forever, would you agree?" "Yeah."

"If all your grandchildren and great-grandchildren were in the room together, what would you say to them about life?"

The old man leans forward and primps his lips. He closes his eyes to think and maybe even to concentrate on such an important answer. He then takes a slight breath, grabs the side of the large armchair, and squeezes it.

"There are a few things that I would tell them for sure. Treat everyone like you would want to be treated. Always tell the truth and do what is right. Now this is me (he points his finger towards me, the interviewer): I have never had a fight with anyone. You must give and take. You know, if someone treats you wrong, you do not have to try and straighten it out. You let the Lord take care of that because it will come back on them if they don't make it right. I guarantee you that. And if you do wrong, it's coming back on you. That is what I want all my children to know. You need to let things slide. It is not your job to fix other people. You cannot straighten another person out, because what he has in him is different from what you have in you. He will pay for all the wrong that he did. And you will pay for the wrong that you did. Do not ever think that you will get away with anything. Many black people in my time believed the reason that the deadly tornado that came through

Waco in 1953 and destroyed most of downtown happened because of what some of the white people did to the young seventeen year old black boy who was accused of murdering a fifty-three year old white woman in 1916. And the reason they thought this is because the tornado ran straight through the same street that they drug the young boy down by his neck before they lynched him. I remember that bad tornado. I was working in the fields that day; me and a lot of other black folks were in the country. We could see the dark clouds rolling in. I still remember looking up and telling everybody that we had better get home because it looked like the weather was going to tear something up. I think Jeanette was with me that day (his oldest child). Red was about three years old at that time (one of his sons). We were miles away from where it touched down and hit the hardest, but we could see the mess it was going to cause. A lot of us quickly jumped in my car and headed to my house. I even had to pull over for a few minutes because I could not see the road that good. The tornado killed a lot of people that day and it destroyed several businesses. It ripped up so much stuff. It killed my aunt Callie's son-in-law because he was at the picture show that day. There was also a guy that had a two-by-four go straight through him. They had to saw it off in the front of him and behind him just to move his body. That wind was blowing fast, hail dropped, and the rain was coming down hard. You could not hardly see anything. It was the worst storm that anyone from down in those parts had ever seen. It destroyed stores, big buildings, and restaurants. It even bent the iron bars of the extension bridge. People lost a lot that day. They lost lives and possessions. I went into town the day after and looked around at what used to be a pretty-hopping town. It was a bad time in Waco. And it took a long time for them to clean up everything and years for them to rebuild. The town had the smell of death on it for a long time too. It looked like something that you would see in a movie. Blackness, smoke, and rubble was everywhere. Yeah, it was rough in '53. I think it was around springtime. Yeah, it was in May I believe. I do not remember what day it was, but it was pretty close to that day in May of 1916 when they lynched that boy. Some people said that it was the woman's husband who killed her and that they laid the blame on the boy who worked on their farm. That is why I am saying, if you do something wrong to some-body it will eventually come back on you. It may not happen until years later, but it will come back around. Those people did wrong by that boy. They knew that he was disabled. Some people said that they tricked him into confessing because he did not know any better. That was a sad day too, for his fam-ily and for black folks. Afterwards, they took his dead body to the black part of town and just left it there for all to see it as an example. You just can't treat people that way." I was quiet because I knew that he meant every word that he spoke.

And he ended it with these words: "If you do what is right in this world, you will make it. My favorite Bible passage are the Ten Commandments. This is the one that stands out to me in Exodus 20:17: 'Honor your father and mother, that your days may be long upon the land which the Lord your God is giving you.'"

(According to Wikipedia.org, Jesse Washington was an African American seventeen- year old farmhand who was lynched in the county seat of Waco, Texas, on May 15, 1916, in what became a well-known example of racially motivated lynch-ing. Washington was convicted of raping and murdering Lucy

THE UNDERSTATEMENT OF PLOWING

Fryer, the wife of his white employer in rural Robinson, Texas. He was chained by his neck and dragged out of the county court by observers. He was then paraded through the street, while being stabbed and beaten, before being held down and castrated. He was lynched in front of Waco's city hall.)

(According to an article written by Ben Cosgrove, on the afternoon of May 11, 1953, an F5 tornado made a direct hit on Waco, Texas. In a matter of minutes, in the face of cyclonic winds that likely topped 300 mph, hundreds of homes and businesses were destroyed, thousands of cars were damaged or totaled; almost 600 people were injured and 114 were killed. It remains one of the deadliest tornadoes in American history.)

"What would make you feel more valued and accepted as a black man in society today?"

"I am ninety-six years old now. I feel pretty good about myself. I do not think I need someone to make me feel valued and accepted. I have lived my life the best way that I know how with whatever I had. I worked hard and raised my children to do the same. And like I said, I am proud of each of them, and I could not have raised a better family. That is good enough for me. God has always carried me.

"I remember when I was a young man and I was supposed to be drafted into the army, but I ended up getting a deferment because I was working these farms for the Boss Man. This was over seventy years ago, so I was in my twenties.

"The way it started was the Boss Man became mad at me one day about some cotton that I was farming on land that I was renting for myself. He was upset because he expected me to be picking his cotton and not my own. But I was working both farms. I did that all the time. So, he decided he was not going to pay me the money that he owed me. He also thought that he would get back at me by canceling my army deferment.

"So, one day the military sent me a letter to come and enlist. But what happened was they sent the letter on the wrong route to the wrong address. Someone else received the letter. The guy that received it lived about eight or nine miles from where my house was. I did not get the letter until 3 o'clock that Saturday evening and I was supposed to leave that Saturday morning. Well, I ended up missing my trip on the bus with all the other guys that were supposed to leave for the army. This put me in a situation where I had to go before the military board to explain why I missed the trip. They asked me if I was farming and I told them that I was. The men who sat at the long table asked me how many bales of cotton I expected to make. And I told them about ten or twelve, give or take. I did not tell them fourteen. That is really what I could do. (We started to laugh knowing that he was wise not to do so.)

They said, 'Well, it looks like you have made a good crop for yourself.'

"I said, 'Yes sir, but I haven't got paid.'

"Then they told me to wait outside while they looked over the letter. So, I went outside and waited for about fifteen to twenty minutes or so. The three men called me back in. They called me 'boy,' you know.

"They said, 'Come in here, boy.'

"I went in there and one of the men picked up the letter and started ripping it up.

"Then he said, 'If we do not send you another letter, don't you ever come back up here. Go finish your crops and get your money.'

"I was shocked and said, 'Thank you, Sir.'

"So, I headed back home. As I was walking, I looked up and the Boss Man was down in there working on the tractor. He was standing down there watching me as I was coming towards him. I walked up to him and he said to me, 'What you doing back here? I thought that you were on that bus.'

"I said, 'No, I went up there and they told me to come back to you so you can pay me my money.'

"He was quiet for a minute."

"I bet he didn't like that, did he?"

"No, he didn't. He had already sold all of my bales of cotton but didn't give me the money."

"Oh, so he was expecting you to go into the army and he would sell all of your crops and keep the profits for himself?"

"Yeah, that was his plan. And when I told him that the military board told me to come back to him and get my money, he said 'Come on and get in this car.' So, I got in the car with him and he took me to the store and gave me my money, all 700 dollars of it. That was a lot of money at that time. And when he gave me the money he said, 'You have to find you some other place to go. You can't live on my farm no more.'

"But what he did not know was that I had already moved. I had still been working for him, but I was not living on his farm. He just did not know it. I had already moved my wife and girls to my daddy-in-law's place across the tracks. So, I told him that I had already moved. And he said, 'What!'

"I repeated, 'I already moved. I don't live on your farm no more.'

"What he tried to do before he canceled my deferment was stand on top of my cotton sack while I was working so that I could not move. It was because it was my own crop. He was okay with me farming his land and picking his cotton, but not okay when it came to my own. When we sold the cotton, we were supposed to divide the profits, but he wanted all the profits for himself, his and mine. The Boss Man wanted it all after all the work that I had done.

"Awhile later, after all that, I was living at my daddy-in-law's place. The Boss Man ended up getting these other guys to work for him. But the problem was he had a place that stayed wet all the time and would never dry up. It was hard for them to break that land. Each time they tried plowing they would get stuck. So, one day he comes over the tracks in his old

1934 Chevy Coupe and he knocks the tailpipe loose from under his car. This was because the car was so low to the ground. "He says to me, 'I knocked my tailpipe loose coming down here to get you.'

"I said, 'What you come to get me for?'

"He said, 'I want you to come and see if you can break that spot of land down there for me.'

"I said, 'Well … yeah, I guess I can.'

"He told me that he had all the rest of them try to do it and none of them could do it.

"I asked him to get me a log chain and the tractor. And I went down there, and I broke that land. Whenever the wheels would start spinning, I would stop and take that chain and hook it onto that plow and move the tractor up, you know … further up from where the spinning was at. Then I would pull it through there. You just had to be patient.

"Yeah, I have seen some tough days in my life, but I tried not to let it get me down. You can't let it get you down."

"What do you think about the Jim Crow law?"

"Well, the Jim Crow law was before my time, and the forty acres and a mule. When I was old enough to know anything about that, my daddy was working on a farm and I was with him all the time. He farmed on a farm for fifty years for one man. Those laws kept us in a certain place."

"Was that his farm?"

"No, it wasn't his farm. It belonged to a doctor. Me and all my siblings were born on that farm (Ennis, Ernest, NC, LC, Alberta, and Lou Annie). Only a few black folks had their own places. The problem was that they could not get the money to farm it. This is the reason a lot of them had to go on the white man's farm."

"So how did your daddy-in-law get his farm?"

"He got his farm from his daddy." Then he began to count on his fingers for a moment.

"Let me see ... there was a lot of them in that family. There was Uncle Rader, Papa Fint (his daddy-in-law), Uncle Gus, and Uncle Irvin, and about two or three girls, that divided up that land. (This property could have been abandoned land after the Emancipation Proclamation or land given to them and it continued to be passed down.)

"So, if freed slaves would have received their forty acres and a mule as promised, then the people who were working the land or farms of others would have actually been working their own land and would have been able to pass that land down to their children, right?"

"Yeah, that's right. There were a few of them that tried to farm, but they just had little garden spots. They just could not get the money from the bank unless they had a place and could tie it up for collateral. That was the only way it may happen.

And even with that, you would still need to go through the Boss Man. Everything went through the Boss Man first."

"Are you okay with these questions?"

"Oh yeah, I think it is important that you ask about history. If young people do not ask, they will lose their history. There has been some good history and some bad history. Back when they lynched that young black boy in 1916 was bad history. Many black people believed that was injustice, the way they killed him. If he did do something wrong, they should have punished him the right way. Not the way that they did. But people do terrible things when terrible things are in their hearts.

"Not all white folks were bad back then. There were some that tried to do right by black folks and that helped."

(According to Wikipedia.org, Jim Crow laws were the number of laws requiring racial segregation in the United States. These laws were enforced in different states between 1876 and 1965. Jim Crow laws provided a systematic legal basis for segregating and discriminating against African Americans. It was a racist term for a black person.)

(As it relates to the "40 Acres and a Mule" that was promised to freed slaves, well it did not happen that way. After President Lincoln approved the Orders No. 15 issued by General William T. Sherman in January 1865 [to confiscate 400,000 acres of coastal property in the south and redistribute it to former slaves in 40-acre plots], on April 15, 1865 Lincoln was assassinated and the new president, Andrew Jackson, revoked the Special Field Orders No. 15. [Georgiaencyclopedia.org].)

"I have decided to stick with love. Hate is too great of a burden to bear." —Martin Luther King Jr.

PART 2

CHAPTER 4

Born Off the Farm

He sat near me on his dark brown leather sofa in front of 75 inches of high definition wondering what he would be asked. His eyes followed me (interviewer) as I scrolled through my notes. Slumped over with a reluctant urgency, he rubbed his prized possessions together. They were the hands that could create, build, and design pretty much anything. And it was those hands that were coupled with his business sense that made him successful in what he did for over 56 years. Ennis Degrate Jr. began his career as a carpenter in the early 1960s. He married at a young age and learned very quickly the importance of establishing and building a firm foundation for his family's sake. The fruit did not fall too far from the tree. Ennis Degrate Jr. is the son of ninety-six-year old Ennis Degrate Sr. Remember the little boy who looked through the hospital window as his father was suffering from Poison Cotton?

Well ... meet Junior. The strong-headed aristocrat that wanted more for himself than what was being offered to black men in the 1960s and '70s. He was sure to break the mold, daring to be different by not accepting conventional handouts of pity and scarce rations. Ennis Jr. was not born on the farm, but he was well acquainted with it. Although he lived on the property owned by his grandfather, he still helped his father on other local farms and cotton fields for years. He learned quickly and observed well as a young boy. Those traits immediately took him on a path of vision and purpose. Now at the age of seventy-three, he ponders on the old days and what it took to journey on a path that was full of mountains and valleys. He walked with a heart of faith and a whole lot of determination, all with the hope that the world must have something better for the black man. It just had to. And if it were out there, he would find it. A candid soul with a lot to say about the world and its erroneous ways of thinking concerning black men, he holds nothing back with a wide-open vent whisking directly into the eyes of falsehood and chipping away at any exaggerated civic virtues held by the standards of American culture. Ennis Jr. had a bit of an edge about him. Maybe because he was not born on a farm. By the time he was born in the 1940s, his family lived on their own property. To him, the "Boss Man" had now become "The Man."

"How did you feel as a child in the 1940s and '50s being black? What were the differences that you noticed in the society?"

"Well, I felt loved by my parents. They did the best they could to raise us up to do what is right. As far as society goes, to a certain extent I thought that slavery was still going on because we still had to chop and pull cotton for the white man. When we went to school, we had split sessions. We went to school six months and was out in the summer for three months. It was basically like this: we were off a month and a half, then we went to the fields in the summer and back to school, then back to the fields. We would get up in the morning by 5 am and start working by 6 am. This was at an early age, like ten or eleven years old. When we had to chop cotton, we chopped from 6 am until 6 pm. And when we pulled cotton, we did it from sunup until sundown. We were given a certain amount we had to pick a day. The money we made went to help take care of our families, of course. For our school clothes, we had to work half a day on Saturdays."

"So, when did you do your homework?"

"In my early years during elementary, we did our homework after all our chores were done. This was after 6 pm. We had to finish in a hurry because we used oil lamps to see our lessons. We did not have electricity. We had to finish before it was too dark at nighttime. For entertainment, we would listen to ballgames on the radio or Roy Rogers (an American country singer and actor). We didn't have televisions at that time, and our radios were battery operated."

"So, are those the differences that you noticed compared to other children your age who were of a different race?"

"Of course, there were more differences. We were going to the fields while they sat at home around their kitchen tables or went on summer vacations. They would be having a good time, going to the swimming pool in the heat of the day being cooled by the water, all the while we were in the dry heated fields picking cotton for their families, making scarce wages. We worked until salty sweat ran down our ankles. People would dream and say, 'You ought to have this education or that job.' But the truth of the matter is that we were too busy trying to survive. Education was basically 'Johnny Come Lately' for those who dreamed of one.

"Like I said, to a certain extent it seemed like slavery. For chopping you were paid $5.00 a day, which was about 50 cents an hour. And for pulling a hundred pounds of cotton you got a dollar and a quarter. If you pulled four or five hundred pounds, you got 6 or 7 dollars. That's on twelve-hour days." "What year was this?"

"This was in the '50s."

(According to the [WHD] Wage & Hour Division US Department, the 1950 minimum wage was 75 cents, and in 1956 it was $1.00 under the Fair Labor Standards Act.)

Black men and women working on farms were receiving half of that, and in some cases less than half.

"After we pulled the cotton, we had to pick up the sacks that were 10 to 12 feet long. We would drag them where they needed to go. There would be painful rings around our shoulders that left scars. And then on our knees we built up hard calluses from kneeling on the ground all day pulling cotton. After picking is when we would drag that large sack of 100 pounds or more to a trailer to weigh it. If no one came to help, we would have to climb up a ladder with the sack on our backs and throw it into the trailer. After which, we would go back down the ladder, tie the sack on the ends, and head back to the fields to start over again. We did the same thing every year until we were old enough to get other jobs, like in a factory or possibly construction. Until then, we were stuck on farms or in the fields. While working in the fields, The Man himself would usually be down the road or up the hill somewhere with binoculars looking down as we worked. If we were caught slacking, the next day we would not have a job. They would say they didn't need us anymore."

"So how did that make you feel?"

"It made me feel less than a man. It made me feel like I was not human with feelings, but more like an object that people used. During those days it was hard on us, especially when we got home after a long day. We could not sleep because we would be extremely sore all over from working. Those cotton bulbs would stick in our hands from pulling them. It was painful. Some people who could afford it had gloves, but some did not. When we got home, we would place our hands in alcohol and rub them to get rid of the soreness. Oh, and our backs would hurt as well. Imagine being a child and you can't lay down in your bed and be comfortable because your back hurt so bad, not to mention you are burning up because the only air you have is the humidity of the Texas heat moving at turtle pace through the windows. "Most of the time we felt dehydrated. While out in the fields they would bring water in a fifty-gallon barrel with a big block of ice in it. Everyone had to drink from the same cup that they passed around at a certain time. We were not allowed to go and get water on our own free will. As children we went to the fields either because our parents took us, or The Man paid someone to pick us up on the back of a Bobtail truck. Some people fell off those trucks and were killed. I can remember them falling between the wagon and the bobtail truck. The trailer would run over them. I saw that happen on several occasions. It was a hard life, you know.

"Now, the system was designed to abuse young black folk, especially those that were in the state of Texas and in the deep South. That is just the way it was. There were certain places that we could not go as teenagers. If we had to go to Waco (city) and we were walking near the known university, the police were going to stop us to see why we were walking that way. There were a lot of places off limits to blacks. People were free, but they really were not FREE. Everything that could be against a black person was against him without any reason except being black."

"What were some of the staple conversations of your time in the 1950s and '60s between black men?"

"We usually talked about trying to make a better living for our families. We wanted to have nice things. In my situation, I really wanted to learn a trade. I wanted to have a skill, so that I could use that skill to bring in finances to take care of my family. Back then, if you went to college, you could be a teacher or a coach. But that was about it. We knew that if you got a business degree in college, we would not get a job in the business field. They just were not going to hire us. Or if you were a scientist or something like that, it would be difficult to be hired. Most blacks that went to college became teachers. That was considered a big-time job. That meant that you were somebody. But even then, black teachers were not making much money.

"I had a black teacher that taught me in school. This was in the mid-1960s. Her check was $550.00 a month. I knew that I needed to make more than that.

"As young black men, we talked about what we could do to make life better. We did not want our children to go through what we had to go through, which I am sure my father felt the same way about me and my siblings. We did not want our children to have books that white children had used for ten to twelve years prior with syrup and all kinds of nasty stuff on them, ripped pages, and all. And then if a black child lost a book, he had to pay full price for the used and outdated book. You see what I'm saying?"

He sat back on his couch contemplating his next thought. He was trying to make sure that we had the complete picture of what he was sharing. Someone had asked him a question and he was not about to hold his tongue in speaking the truth. He was nearly seventy-four years old. He had nothing to lose. And so, he continued …

"Some of my friends worked two and three jobs to try and get ahead. Most of us left where we grew up and went to other areas to work or to learn a trade.

"I left the area where I grew up to learn a trade (less than 100 miles or so outside of Waco, Texas). I went to Austin, Texas for four years. That is where I learned how to hang sheet rock. I would get up in the mornings and leave home around 4 am and get to Austin around 5 am, eat breakfast, and be on the job by 6 am. I was already raising a family, so I had to do something. We had to leave Austin by 4 pm in the evening so that we would be home around 6 or 6:30 pm. I did the same thing every day, five days a week, for four years.

"After that, I was able to settle into my job at a local company just miles from where I lived, and this is where I made a comfortable living for my family."

"Are you content with the way society has treated black men?"

"No, I am not content. If you are a young black man, there are so many challenges that you must fight through. You must work extremely hard to have a better life. When you have black children, you need to make sure that they have a good work ethic and that they understand there is a place that some people in society expect them to stay in. What do I mean by that? Well it's like this: when I was a young man if I passed a white person on the street or in a public place, especially a female, I had better look the other way and not speak to her or I just may find myself hanging from a tree or beaten in the worst way. Sometimes when I think about my younger days, I start to cry. No human beings should have to live the way black men had to live, from my great-grandfather, grandfather, and my father. We had many challenges. I know every generation is different, but more of the same is taking place. We have seen this with all the brutal killings that have taken place in the last five to ten years in America involving young unarmed black men and law enforcement. The death toll continues to rise as many are walking around pretending that this is not a problem. Parents are losing their young sons prematurely. This is sad to think about. Civil authorities are put into place to protect and uphold the law. I do not believe all law enforcement officers have wrong intentions. Many do their jobs well and we are thankful for them. But something needs to be done about our broken system and the ones who infiltrate to corrupt it. It is The Man all over again in an immediate pursuit to eliminate on the grounds of 'Being Black.' They tried back then, and they continue to try now.

"And then if you tried to have something back in my day, they would be waiting in the shadows to take it away or try to pull you down. That is just the way things were. Why did we have to go through all of that? Why are we as black men still dealing with so much loss? When I say 'they,' I mean those who intentionally wanted to hurt black folks.

"I remember going to a small grocery store as a young man, and the name of the store was Bob's. I walked in the store and needed items from behind the counter. I said, 'Bob, can you give me that over there.' And he turned and replied, 'There is no Bob here, nigger!' Horrible memory is etched in his mind.

"That is the type of life the young black men lived daily when I was young. You really had to mind your P's and Q's because Bob was in control of the groceries that you and your family needed during the winter. If you said something out of the way or smart to Bob, he could deny you credit for food during the winter months when it was most needed. (Most blacks did not work fields in winter and needed store credit to get them through.) They had a way of adding unnecessary interest to your bills too. You knew you were paying more for your groceries than everyone else. Most of the time, blacks did not receive actual money for their work: they worked for their food. Most of them did not own properties either— they lived on the Boss Man's farm (which at the time was nothing more than a modern-day plantation). If you did not work for him, you could not live on the property, understandably so. But for most ex-slaves, their children, and grandchildren, that was the only life they knew. They had never been anywhere else, done anything else, or seen anything else. They had always worked for whatever and however the Boss Man wanted to pay them.

"Now, I know that we live in a different time and things are better for us in society, but I tell about those times so that people can get a better understanding of why black people sometimes think and respond to certain things in a particular way. You cannot speak into the struggle unless you know the struggle firsthand."

(According to Merriam-Webster's Dictionary, the "N" word is an insulting and contemptuous term for a black person.)

"The soul that is within me no man can degrade." —Frederick Douglas

CHAPTER 5

An Unfair Deal

"Have you ever been made to feel inferior to another race, particularly the white race?"

"Yes, I believe all black folks at one time or another have been made to feel inferior to whites. In those days, they made sure you knew that the system was made to work in their favor and that made us feel like second-class citizens. Believe it or not, it still happens today. So how far have we really come? "For example, if you went to a bank for a loan, they would quickly turn you down. But if you took a white man with you, the bank would be more apt to give you money. They did not value your word, but they valued his word. For some, all they had to do was pick up the phone and call the bank on your behalf and that would be just as good. It is still that way today. When we built our church (he is a deacon of a local black Baptist church now), it cost a little less than a million dollars. This was in 2004. We went to the bank that we have always dealt with. We had $600,000.00 in that bank. We as a church leadership, we requested a loan for $400,000.00. The deacons of our church had a very substantial personal net worth as well, but that did not matter to the bank. They still would not lend us the money to build the new church. They told us that we needed to build the church in sections and pay as we go until it was completed. That bank had $600,000.00 of ours for over ten years. They were making money with our money and yet they refused to loan us a dime. That is the way they operated. This is what I meant when I said that The Man was always waiting in the shadows to try and take it away or to pull you down. You know, keep you from moving forward or getting ahead.

"We eventually left that bank after twenty-five years of history with them and went to another bank. The other bank was eager to give us a loan. They stated that it was because of the outstanding collateral that we had. That is the difference between some rural banks and some city banks. It was the skewed mentality of rural bank employees. They had thoughts like, 'What are they doing with that kind of money anyway?'

As if we had no business with it. And this is what gave them the right in their own minds to deny us.

"I hope and pray that one day this type of behavior will stop. But until then, it is full force ahead."

"If you could tell other races what it feels like to be a black man, what would you say?"

"I would tell them to watch the movie *When They See Us* (a recent movie on black injustice); this is an example of what has been happening to black men for years. There are still many black men who are in prison unjustly today. Look at the black people who have went through the criminal justice system. Some of them are supposed to be there for their crimes, but there are some who are there that have been wrongly accused. Many of them did not receive good representation. A white man and a black man can commit equal crimes. And there are times when a black man will get 40 to 50 years and the white man will get a probated sentence. That is an unfair deal.

"I would like for a white person to get up in the morning and paint his or her face black and go into the local grocery market or the local courthouse to do business. This will be a head-on experience of racial bias. In this day in age it may only be hinted at, but sometimes it is still there. They can test it even further if they go home, remove the paint, and go back to the same places. The level of respect will then heighten to some degree. All in all, this treatment has only made the black race stronger because we had to endure so many things.

"There are a lot of white men that I consider my brothers. I have known them for years and we have a good relationship. But deep down inside, there is this thought that if something comes up where you have a black person on one side and a white person on the other side, nine times out of ten all bets will be in the white person's favor if they are the majority. Even if they are as wrong as two left shoes. Now this is just the way my mind has been shaped to believe.

"Maybe things have gotten better. I hope they have. But it was not that long ago that I went to the local courthouse and spoke to the district judge about the problem based on the number of black men being incarcerated versus the number of white men for the same offenses. I was curious why black men were getting all the prison time while white men who had committed crimes were still walking the streets." "What was his reply?"

"He said that he noticed it in the small city where we lived but did not know why. He mentioned that maybe they were not getting good attorneys. I met with him two or three times to discuss it, and nothing really changed. White man steals the chicken and he gets to go home and eat the chicken. Black man steals the chicken and he gets twenty years. Is that fair?"

He looks at us with a straight face and did not blink an eye. He meant those exact words. And who were we (interviewer and cameraman) to dispute it? These were his experiences, not ours. This is the mind of one black man.

"So how did you stay out of the system?"

"I stayed out of the system as a young black man because I quickly learned the system. I knew what it was about. My daughter was about five years old (which was around 1970) when the Klan chased me home and ran me off the road with both of my small children in the car."

"Really? Why did they chase you?"

"Because they knew who I was. They were the same people that I worked on the job with. Some of them were different people after hours. When they got off work, they became Klansmen. Their personalities changed when the sun went down. You could not trust anyone. You just had to learn how to deal with folks. You had to be straight up, so they knew where you stood. I will tell you something else that happened to me as a young man. They tried and they tried ..."

"They tried what?"

"In 1964 I worked while I was still in school. Sometimes I worked around The Man's (my boss) property near his company. One day, I was working around his swimming pool and there were a few white girls hanging at the pool having a good time. I saw them there, but I continued to do my work. The Man (my boss) was out of town. That weekend someone broke into The Man's house and stole things. Every white person in the neighborhood swore that it was me. No one stood up for me, so I had to stand up for myself. When the sheriff came, he pulled up in a 1964 Chevy. It was snuff brown with a long antenna on the back of it. He whooped up in the horseshoe driveway of The Man's house. I stood there working in the rock garden that day. He walked up to me and said, 'Hey, you been in that house over the weekend?'

"I replied, 'Yeah.'

"He said again, 'You went in that house?' Gesturing towards the front door of the house.

"I replied in turn, 'Yeah, I went in there.'

"'Did you knock that patio door out?'

"'No.'

"'How did you get in the house then?'

"I dug in my pocket and I pulled out keys to everything. Then I answered, 'I have the keys.'

"The sheriff looked at me with stern eyes and cursed at me. Then he looked at my boss and said, 'You mean to tell me this boy has keys to everything around here?' "And my boss answered, 'Yeah, he has the keys to everything.' "I had keys to the gates, the house, the cars—everything.

"Then the sheriff said, 'I'll be damned!' Then he quickly got back into his snuff-brown '64 Chevy and drove off. And that was the last time I heard of that."

"That was it?"

"Yep, that was it because he figured if The Man gave me the keys to everything around his house, I must be something special. But if it had been left up to the neighbors, I would have been locked up. These same people had watched me grow up when I was a kid. They knew what kind of person I was. They knew I came from a good family. But I had got what they called 'Besides Myself' (uppity). This was because I was thinking for myself and trying to figure out how to make a better living. How to be somebody. I was not just going to the fields every day chopping and pulling cotton on their farms like they expected black men to do. I quit that when I turned sixteen.

"They labeled so many black people back then and they were good people. They treated you like you were less than they were. They had a habit of calling a black woman 'GAL' and a black man 'BOY.' This was in their efforts to depreciate our value. I looked at my dad one time (Ennis Degrate Sr.) and said, 'Daddy, why do you let them talk to you that way? You are forty years old and the person talking to you cannot be much older than seventeen. He should be saying "Yes, Sir" to you, not the other way around.

He should not be calling you "BOY." That's not right.'

Ennis Sr. accepts H

"My daddy said, 'Well, I got what I wanted and that is what's important.'

"What that said to me was sometimes you need to climb down off the ladder to get what you want instead of reaching from the top. If it had been me, I would not have received anything because I would not have been able to compose myself the way my dad did. I understood that he had to do what was necessary to survive. He was thinking of his family the whole time. Because back in those days, you did not talk back to a white man, no matter their age. And if you tried to defend yourself, you could end up in a lot of trouble, if you know what I mean."

"You are one of the few African American men in this country or black or whatever you prefer to be called that has a father that is still alive at the age of ninety-six. That itself is a treasure from heaven, don't you think?"

"Yes, it is. I am proud of my dad. He is a good man. And the only time he was ever in jail was the time that he hit a stop sign. We were driving in town (Waco) on Bosque Street. I was a young boy then. I remember my dad made too sharp of a turn and the car hooked the side of a stop sign. It was an accident. My dad drove a few feet up the street to move out of the way of cars waiting behind him and pulled over to a curve. The people saw when he hit the sign and they called the police. The police came and picked him up for 'Hit & Run.' Can you believe that? He had to pull the car up because part of the post from the sign was under the wheel of his car. This happened in 1962. He had to spend a few hours in jail until someone bailed him out. I am sure that the sign had been hit before. It was too close to the curb anyway. And if it were hit by a white person, a warning or a ticket would have probably been given.

"So, speak to my generation. I am in my fifties. I can look a white man or white woman in his or her eyes. And I do not have to cross the street without saying anything. I can say 'hello' and ask him or her how they are doing without fear of it being misinterpreted. At least I would hope it is not misinterpreted. Then there is a generation coming after me, like my son. What would you say to the next generation that we call the millennials?"

"I would tell them to respect and appreciate those who have paved the way for them. They can now do things that we were forbidden to do, yet we pressed through under tough circumstances.

"I would tell them to please get an education or learn a trade. Do something that will help them take care of their families. When they make good money, invest it wisely so when they leave this earth, they leave something behind for their sons and daughters that come behind them. The key to the wealth of black people is the fathers leaving their children an inheritance. Then in turn, they can leave their children an inheritance. And the cycle will continue for generations to come. That is the head start that is needed. I knew this guy named 'Newspaper George.' He took a liking to me. I would give him a cigarette when he would ask me for one (years ago when I smoked). I knew him because he built houses. He would always give me a watermelon Jolly Rancher candy (go figure). He was a Jewish guy. He also ran the *Waco News Tribune* at one time. One day he said, 'Hey Ennis, you know why black people can't get ahead?'

"I said, "No, I don't know, Mr. George."

"He said, 'Because when their parents pass away, they never have anything to leave their children. A Jewish man will always leave his children twice as much as his parents left him. Now, that is how you get ahead.'

"What he said made sense to me. If it does not happen that way, our families will always struggle. "The other thing that I would tell other young black men is do not have a bunch of kids if you know that you cannot take care of them. I tell the young folk all the time that they will regret it if they do. It is a sad thing that keeps being passed down from generation to generation. I think some whites get an enjoyment of seeing young black people in line at the grocery store with food stamps or standing in line trying to get financial assistance to pay bills. They expect it because that is how some of them see black people. Many still believe blacks are second-class citizens, anyway. Do not get me wrong, there is nothing wrong with having a family and there is nothing wrong with having a lot of children, but do not have ten or fifteen kids if you only make $20,000.00 a year. The children will suffer if this happens. Have as many as you are able to take care of. Do things in a decent way. Get a college education or learn a useful trade first. This will help you take care of a family. Here is what my dad told me. I will never forget it.

"He said, 'Junior, never promise your child something you know you cannot give them. If you tell your child that he or she can have this or that, please be prepared to give it to them, especially if you want your child to respect you as the head of the family.' And so, I have always tried to do that. I will honor what I said I would do.

"Proverbs 13:22 says, 'A good man leaves an inheritance to his children's children, but the wealth of the sinner is stored up for the righteous' (NKJV).

"'Start where you are with what you have. Make something of it and never be satisfied.' —George Washington Carver"

"What would make black men feel more valued and accepted in society today?"

low expectations b/c of history

"I know that I won't see it in my lifetime, but one of the things they can do is accept a person for who he is, treating him right and fairly. I am not even sure if you will see it in your lifetime, but I hope so. The reason for that is ancestry. The 'good ole boy' system works in this country. We have the 'Haves & Have Nots.' Why would they change something they think is working, especially if it is working for them? "America was built on the backs of those considered second-class citizens. They treated black people like each of us were a number. A hundred years ago, you were considered a quarter of a person. Do you know how many people were affected by what happened a hundred years ago? Some of those people are still living and their grandchildren are as well. I talk to my grandchildren all the time, especially the young men. I tell them about what happened in the 1940s and '50s. I am passing true history down to them. Why not? The white man is passing his history down to his children and grandchildren. Hopefully, we can all come together and hash some things out. With God all things are possible. Like I said, we can hope. We need to find a way to unify."

"So, what is the remedy for it?"

"The remedy is to LOVE people, EDUCATE yourselves and your families, TRY different things and if it doesn't work, try something else. GIVE every person a fair chance no matter the color their skin or what side of the tracks they come from.

DO right by others. Just do not give up, otherwise it is like a curse that keeps repeating itself.

"A hundred years' curse is a bad thing. I am not saying that the curse is on blacks or whites, I am saying it is a curse on society and how it sees people. We need to get into position to help one another. Black business owners should be hiring qualified black employees. I keep hearing what the Unemployment Department is doing for black people. The Unemployment Department is not doing anything. For black people, unemployment has not changed in fifty years. They just want you to believe that. All that is happening is they are taking black people off the unemployment roll. They do not keep accurate records of who signed up and who did not. Black unemployment is high. How is it possible to have a business of a hundred people and not have at least one black employee? Or even have a business of 500 employees and only 1% are black? Tell me how this works if there are no racial biases and things are fair? Companies need to be challenged to rethink their hiring process and methods to attract and maintain a diverse workplace environment. We are a diverse society, right?

"Unemployment is probably at eight or nine percent for blacks right now, while the rest of the country is saying that it is at three and a half percent. This just is not true. What the system has done is made people, especially in America, believe a lie over the truth and that is because no one wants to hear the truth.

(According to Statista, in 2019, the unemployment rate of African Americans in the USA stood at 6.1 percent. This was over 1.6 times the national average of 3.7 percent.)

"I worked for the same company for fifty-six years. When I started, there weren't any blacks working in this company."

"So, you worked fifty-six years for the same company, you retired as an executive, and you were a mayor of a city for twelve years? This means you are not speaking out of hearsay, but actual experience, right?"

"Yes, I am talking from experience. I also served as president of the school board for ten years."

"So why didn't you make the change?"

"I felt like I helped advance some things as much as I could with the resources that I had. But it is going to take more than one ordinary person in a small town to change things in a big world. When I was in a position of authority in the company where I worked, I hired minorities and taught them the same skills that I had.

"I hired my brothers, my cousins and brothers-in-law. I taught them how to hang sheet rock and to build. This helped them make a living for their families. Some of them left years later and started their own companies. I continued to keep minorities employed in the company.

"I started at the company in 1962. I was about sixteen years old. I worked my way up the ranks. And this all began in that small rock garden where I was accused of stealing.

"There was a time when we had twenty to twenty-five black people working there at the same time because I hired them,

Hispanics as well. When I retired in 2016, there were only three black people remaining in the company for whatever reason. Black men helped build businesses to become successful and profitable entities back in the day and today they are being replaced by non-black men. This happens all the time in America. Do you think this is progress? We take five steps forward and then ten steps back. Our value in society has been proven many times over. That is not the problem. The problem is the acknowledgment of that value by society. We fight and work hard for everything that we get.

"I am grateful for the distance that black men have come in America, but we still have a long way to go. Do I put my trust in a society that has promised to FOSTER every human being? No, I do not. I challenge every person to answer this question: 'How has society fostered black men?' I put my trust in God and Him alone. He is the one that has given His all for me. My life Bible verse is John 3:16, 'For God so loved the world that He gave His one and only Son, that whoever believes in Him shall not perish but have eternal life' (NIV). That is what I put my trust in."

(According to Oxford languages, the definition of FOSTERING means to encourage or promote the development of.)

> **"The ultimate measure of a man is not where he stands in moments of comfort and convenience, but where he stands at times of challenge and controversy."** —Martin Luther King Jr.

PART 3

CHAPTER 6

A Cause for Justice

Always on the go making things happen for the kingdom of God is what he does. I know him to be a man whose steps are ordered, going only where he is led to go. Finally taking a moment to just breathe and collect the thoughts that lie just below the fine surface of his heart. He sat up sternly in his chair at the kitchen table with tightly clasped hands, anxiously awaiting the questions that would cause him to dig deep into his core and gather the bits and pieces that mattered to him most. He is tall and lean with a disposition that seems strong and full of assurance. He would be the one in the room that everyone thought they knew or wanted to know. His stature can be captivating, and he seems to have a knack that draws you in. He looks to be a natural born leader with plenty to say about the past, present, and future. He is a former professional athlete that understands the concept of teamwork and a pastor who believes in hope and walks by faith. I did not want the interview to be too formal so I decided to lean back in my chair in hopes that he would follow my lead. He slowly unclasped his hands, but that was as far as he would follow. I could tell that he had been around the block more than a few times. He had learned a lot about life in the fifty-four years that he had been on earth. The ups and downs of being a man. The highs and lows of being a black man. How did they even compare? I knew that his experiences, both good and bad, would be worth the time and effort put into the interview. Questions asked would immediately become the key that would open the gates to words that have waited to escape the prison of silence. A silence that has been locked by poise and steadiness for years in regards for others.

When his words made their way into the atmosphere, I knew that I had to be ready. I was prepared to capture them with the ink of a pen and the pure surface of yearning paper. They would not be lost by the wayside. They meant something. Words accumulated and written are never wasted. Someone will read them and someday pages will turn for the greater good.

I fully expected his words to burst into flames with one agenda: CAUSE AND EFFECT. This man would speak in terms that simplify the voice of reason and change in a society that rambles on about desiring both. There is a story to tell in all of us. This day was all about his story and the experiences that shaped his heart and mind. As a pastor, he would tell his story if only to save one. As a black man, he would tell his story if only to influence many. As a man, he would tell his story if only to help transform the heart of a nation that has repeatedly declared, "We the people ..." And so, with every vessel of my heart I listened, and with unrestrained passion he gracefully released words into the atmosphere to be recorded forever. And in his confidence, he believes that someone would read them and someday pages would turn for the greater good.

"How did you feel as a child in the late 1960s and 1970s being black? What differences did you notice?"

"Well, no one ever explained to me that I was part of one of the first generations that was desegregated in schools. When I was in kindergarten, we were the first class going through the process of desegregation. I thought that it was normal to be in class with other children of a different race. It was not necessarily the other children that made me feel different, it was more so the teachers and school authorities. It seemed normal to me. I just thought they were having a bad day and taking it out on me and other black children. It was not until I was a little older that I realized there was racism happening. I remember being in a class with only one other black person and the rest were white, along with a white teacher. Many of the other classes were filled with all black students and black teachers. This was their way of dividing us up or SEGREGATING in the center of INTEGRATION. But somehow, I was placed as a minority in a class full of whites. I guess that was due to the hand of God on my life to help me become more diverse in my thinking. I just did not know it at the time. I think growing up I experienced racial bias more economically than anything else. There was a mindset of some whites to pay you lower wages if they thought that you did not know any better. Although some blacks took what they could get, others did not accept what they were offered because they knew that it was not fair. I could see the difference economically in how I lived as a child versus how some white children lived, but I was grateful for my family and all the hard work that my mother did to take care of her five children. She did what she could with the hand she was dealt. We did not share in the same privileges that some of the white people in our area enjoyed, and I am sure it had nothing to do with who worked the hardest. As I became older, I understood the system of BLACK CODES that began way before my time but were still very prevalent in the south.

"My mom worked three jobs to support and take care of us. We were raised to be strong, self-sufficient, and to do right by others. Before I was born, my mother moved to California after a disagreement that she and her mother had related to a relationship that she was in with a man that she loved in Texas. She and my two sisters made a home there. She then met a man in California and became pregnant with me. A little while later she found out that he was already married. She was disappointed about the situation. Several months after I was born, she moved back to Texas and eventually married her Texas love and we became a blended family. At that time, she had three children and he had five (the five did not live with us). We moved to a small country town in Texas. My mother and stepfather had two children together a few years later. So, there were five children in the house daily. Needless to say; I grew up in the type of environment that had a lot of stress and a lot of strife all the time. Not to mention the pressures of society outside of the home, especially for a black person trying to make it. We had this stepfather/stepchildren clash going on most of the time. It was hard. My stepfather never held a consistent job. He did odd and end jobs. My mother was my example. She was the one who held it down. She worked at a hotel making very, little money. She drove a school bus. And she cleaned houses for people in the community. At the same time, I would help my step-grandfather with his lawn-care business (I was the middle child, but the oldest son). This is how I learned the principle of doing business. It was my first encounter of doing business with people of a different race. When I became older and my step-grandfather passed away, those same people wanted me to take over the little business. The only problem was they were not willing to pay me what they knew they should and what was fair. This taught me not to trust them. My mother taught me the value of hard work and what to expect from it. I cannot remember us as a family ever receiving any government handouts. My mother was opposed to that. She was not going to be responsible for raising a generation that relied on the government. She raised us to rely on the word of God, our gifts, and talents that God had given us, along with a good work ethic. I am grateful that I had a strong woman in my life as a parent. I have since seen some men and women from that same community who did not have parents with those strong values. They relied heavily on handouts. I am not saying that there is anything wrong with receiving help. Everyone needs help at one time or another. I am saying to completely rely on a system to take care of you your entire life is not right, especially if you are able physically and mentally to care for yourself. Complete government assistance is not always beneficial, sometimes it can be a hindrance to you as a person and to us as a people. Something originally put in place to help people has now become another source of control. I have seen generations of children being raised up with an entitlement spirit simply because there was a lack of discipline and convictions."

"Was it difficult at times?"

"Yes, it was but we made it through. There were times that we had to go without and there were times that we had enough. Although there were significant economical differences among races in my younger days, I was still proud of my upbring-ing while living in the small Texas town and attending school there. "Here is the reality in terms of differences. As a people, African Americans have come a long way in this country. The problem is that even in coming a long way, there continues to be stipulations and dividing lines. After the Emancipation Proclamation, a plethora of laws were put into place to con-trol and dictate lives of FREE men and women. For example, Black Codes (Black Laws) which were mainly used in the south to restrict blacks. These laws basically compartmental-ized blacks. They listed where blacks could live, work, shop, and so forth. You know, a designated compartment. If you are mixed in with everyone else (the white race), there could be a problem. And although Black Codes were finally abolished in 1964 due to Civil Rights, some mentalities were not.

"I remember about three years ago while living in North Carolina, my wife and I went to visit some college friends who were living in the Charlotte area. Now full disclosure to my next statement. Our friends are a beautiful, well-to-do white couple living in a very affluent neighborhood that looked to be an original prominent area. Our college friends are very down-to-earth people and as honest as the day is long. We have known them for thirty-plus years.

"During our visit, we sat on their back patio enjoying grilled steaks and salad, laughing about the good old days. Then our friends began telling us about their plans to renovate the small guest house that was in their backyard. They were trying to decide on contractors. The next thing that came out of their mouths completely shocked me and my wife. They told us that before they could have any work done to the property, they had to go back and look at their original house purchase contract and deed. Reading over it once again, they saw something that they did not notice when they first bought the house, which was probably in 2014. But through the years, the original deed basically had a clause (Restrictive Covenant) that prohibited blacks from ever buying the property. No doubt this was placed in the deed by the first owners. We could not believe what we were hearing. The lengths that people went through to keep blacks in their place years ago are unbelievable. This was how they covered all their bases, clearly not leaving any stones unturned. It was not just well-to-do areas it was any area where the white race was the majority. It was just more of the same, controlled segregation."

(According to Deep Blue University of Michigan, Racially Restrictive Covenants were widespread tools of discrimination used by white homeowners to prevent the migration of people of color into their neighborhoods during the first half of the 20th century.)

(According to KhanAcademy.org in [article] "Reconstruction": Southern states enacted Black Codes after the Civil War to prevent African Americans from achieving political and economic autonomy.)

(According to Britannica.com-Black-Code: Reconstruction did away with Black Codes, but after Reconstruction ended in 1877, many of their provisions were enacted in the Jim Crow laws, which were not finally done away with until passage of the Civil Rights Act of 1964.)

"What were the staple conversations of black men in your teens to early twenties?"

"Our conversations were usually about a CAUSE. And if there was not a cause at the time, we would discuss fishing, sports, girls, and homework. When there was a cause worth standing up for, we stood. Like the time I was in high school and we had a white football coach who did not like blacks. In fact, he really looked down on us. He was also the Athletic Director, so he had a lot of influence in the small 3A school that I attended. One day after football practice, an athlete on our team finished up his shower in the locker room and left for the day. Because he forgot something in the locker room, he returned later to get it. This was after everyone else was supposedly gone. When he went back into the field house, he overheard three white coaches making derogatory remarks (one main coach using the 'N' word, no doubt about some of the players). Needless to say; the young man was devastated and traumatized after hearing this from the mouth of a coach. Today it would be called PTSD (post-traumatic stress disorder).

"He shared with his parents and teammates what was said, and it became a very, big ordeal. All the black athletes rallied together and demonstrated 'A Walk Out.' That is the only time I can remember in my childhood when there was a real serious 'Cause for Justice.' We banded together not only as athletes, but as a community. The coach was eventually fired by the school. They hired another coach who was more sympathetic and understanding to the needs of African Americans. He treated all of us equal.

"Teachers, school authorities, and coaches spend more than eight hours a day with children. They are entrusted to not only teach, but to help guide children in the right direction. When something is not pure and healthy about that, it becomes very distorted and the children suffer. Who knows to what extent?

"As black people, I think we can sense when someone of a different race is fake or not authentic towards us. It is like a built-in radar that is being constantly tuned. The longer we live the more fine- tuned it becomes.

"The whole nation of the United States is the perfect example of enforced integration. I think that from the beginning, God our creator intended for this country to be diverse, unlike any other nation. We all know the history of the 1950s and '60s and the civil rights movement. Everything God does, He does according to a pattern based on His kingdom principles. The principles that He established have not changed and never will. One of the principles that He set up are the three ordained authorities. They are parental, spiritual, and civil. The first being parental authority is discussed in the Bible in Ephesians 6:1. It simply says, 'Children obey your parents in the Lord for this is right.' This authority is the first that most people will contend with. The second are the spiritual authorities. The Bible clearly gives us a picture of who are considered the spiritual authorities in the land. Hebrews 13:17 says, 'Obey those who rule over you and be submissive for they watch out over your soul as those who must give an account. Let them do so with joy and not grief.' These are our pastors and leaders in the church. Then last but not least are the civil authorities. Romans 13:1 reads, 'Let your soul be subject to governing authorities for there is not authority except from God.' And of course, our civil authorities are those who uphold the laws in our states, cities, and communities (police officers, judges, mayors, governors, and so forth).

"In the 1960s during the civil rights movement, there was so much tension going on because of rebellion against God's ordained authorities. It is funny how the devil is always trying to use God's patterns against Him. He took civil authorities that were set up to do right by the people and caused them to rebel against an integrated society. A greater authority being the United States government had to soon step in and enforce the desegregation process because of the 14th Amendment. It was recognized that segregation was unconstitutional. This process had to be particularly pushed throughout the south because they did not want to submit to an integrated society.

"Now fast-forward into 1969 when I was sitting in an integrated classroom. We as children did not know that we were products of an enforced integration. Just like there had to be a governing body for the United States as a whole, there also had to be governing boards for smaller cities and towns like the one that I grew up in. The so-called leaders there did not want to submit to the desegregation guidelines. They really did not want change. They wanted to keep us separated. What was the point of keeping us separated? They resisted integration so much so that they implemented their own rules and guidelines for it, instead of following the state guidelines. This was all a part of the old Jim Crow law way of thinking. People like Dr. Martin Luther King Jr. had given their lives and sacrificed so much in the name of EQUALITY AND CHANGE. But the way many of them thought was that we could have equal opportunities among ourselves, but we were not granted the equality in participating on the same playing fields of our white counterparts. We all knew that their school buildings were better, their resources were better, and their all-around opportunities for good education was better. Every person from the surrounding areas near the small town in Texas where I grew up should read some of the articles that give history concerning where we lived. It may give them a better understanding of why some mindsets and old ways of thinking may still be embedded there. The average citizen may not know some of its history. If my memory serves me correctly, I believe there were twenty-two black students that initially transferred and integrated into two white schools after the desegregation process began in that town. They were part of a partial integration. They were from the B/W school. I think that those twenty-two students should be honored. First, it could not have been easy to move from their element into an environment that possibly was not the most welcoming. And I am sure they had to quickly adjust to an atmosphere where many odds were against them. They deserve acknowledgment for being the FIRST. This is an important part of history.

"I can tell you this: I spent years running up and down the basketball courts of the middle school and high school in that small town, even years after the 'Walk Out' demonstration. I went to college on a scholarship and went even further as a professional basketball player for ten years abroad in the FIBA league (Europe and South America). There has only been one time that the school has ever recognized me as a professional athlete from that town, and that was because a black coach who knew me personally invited me to come and speak to students at the middle school assembly. Other than that, no one there has ever acknowledged that I was the FIRST basketball player to continue my career at the professional level, becoming part of the one percent that elevated to that ranking. In fact, both my brother and I became professional athletes. What are the chances of that—two professional athletes from the same family that attended the same school? Sometimes I wonder if we were of a different race if they would have named a street after one of us or asked us to speak during a graduating commencement. I mean, you must wonder. I am now a pastor and it amazes me that I have traveled around the world and have spoken in various arenas, yet the very place where sports began for me chooses to disregard that I was even there. Although I have kept moving forward, it still makes me wonder. Reminiscing back to my school days and my time as an athlete certainly puts things into perspective. Even the thought of justice and all the causes that I believed in as a young man had its level of importance when you look at the bigger picture. Banding together made a big difference back in those days, whether it was those who had to integrate for the FIRST time or those who had to stand up, rally together, and demonstrate for the FIRST time.

"There have been many times in my life that I have stood up for what I believed to be RIGHT. And in those times, the price was costly. I had to boycott some things and confront many things. So, demonstrating 'A Walk OUT' as a kid was just the beginning for me."

(According to the Omeka.net [The Mansfield Crisis], approximately 28 schools had announced plans for complete or partial integration by August 18, 1955. Of the first districts were San Antonio, Austin, and Corpus Christi. Many smaller populated cities and towns followed.)

(According to the article "A Brief History of Groesbeck ISD" compiled by William F. Reagan, he wrote, "Integration was slow to come to Groesbeck ISD. After the passage of the Civil Rights Act in 1964, Groesbeck ISD created a "Freedom of Choice" policy. Under this policy complete freedom to transfer was supposed to be allowed any time within the district prior to the opening day of the school year. In 1966, a six-member team from the Department of Health, Education, and Welfare visited Groesbeck and determined that Groesbeck ISD was not in compliance with the Civil Rights Act." Because of reasons including discrepancies in carrying out the "Freedom of Choice" policy. It was not until 1968 that the school board adopted a plan for total integration that began with the 1969–1970 school year.)

"Injustice anywhere is a threat to justice everywhere." —Martin Luther King Jr.

CHAPTER 7

Perceptions

"Are you content with the way society has treated men of color?"

"No, of course not. High blood pressures, heart attacks, and strokes are just a few to describe the type of stress that men have been under; now add being black to that equation. I can tell you as a black man that has

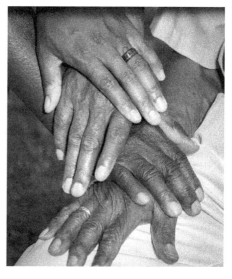

seen and done a lot in my fifty-four years of life, it is a daily battle. You are under constant scrutiny and surveillance, with subtle interrogations. Your IQ is always in question, or as they call it these days, your EQ (emotional intelligence) is in question, and any other kind of Q you can think of can be in question. These are not bitter statements—these are actual true statements. I have sat in meetings with other professionals (being the only man of color in the room) and proposed a God-given idea and no one paid any attention to that idea. It was as though I said nothing. Then forty-five minutes later, another professional (of another race) will propose the same idea, and it is accepted as this amazing revelation. Now we have just wasted forty-five minutes because no one wanted to admit the idea I proposed was good. What I have learned is that it is never the ideas (package), but rather the deliverer. I have dealt with this more times than I can count. Sometimes it is almost easier to dummy-down. Unfortunately, that is not in my nature. When you have good intentions and just want to help, it can be misconstrued as trying to take over, and that is far from the truth. I have never tried to take over. I have only tried to use my gifts and talents to help out in the best possible way. That is why God put me there.

"There are misperceptions (mistaken beliefs) of the black man all over the world in different places. I have been dealing with these wrong perceptions from the times of grade school and college, to my time spent in the marketplace and churches. At some point, I am thinking that misconceptions should have played out by now, but it's human nature I suppose. Let us just 'Cut to the Chase.' Ask me who I am, and I will tell you. Pursue a relationship with me and find out my story. Appreciate my differences and respect me as a person. Get to know me before judging me and creating your own false conclusions about me. Why allow the color of someone's skin to be the initial implicit bias against him?

"I can sum it up like this. Most recently I spoke with a mayor of a prominent city. I asked him, 'What are the two things that are constantly on your heart about your city?'

"He told me that it is the safety of the police officers in the city, and secondly, minorities who get caught up in the cycle where they do not have the economic means to pay the smallest of fines. They can be pulled over for a busted taillight on their vehicle while driving to work, and when the officer runs his tags, he makes a discovery. Unfortunately, he finds out that the person has other unpaid citations issued years before back when he did not have the means to even get to the courthouse or pay the citations. The fees only continued to stockpile. The officer sees this and immediately takes him to jail. Now he is caught in a system that began with a petty infraction. Not only are black men caught in this system, but young Latinos and whites are as well. But the statistics are higher for young black men."

"Why are you personally not content?"

"Because it could be my son, my grandson, or even my nephew. I do not want them unjustly accused or even justly accused with unfair consequences. Once you are in the system, it is difficult to get out of the system. It could end up being twenty or thirty years of their lives. That is a hopeless place to be in. Many young black men have found themselves in this place.

"I have traveled to forty-eight states, visited eighteen different countries, and lived in six of those countries. My horizons have been broadened to say the least. When I traveled abroad in the late 1980s to the late 1990s, I realized the perceptions of black men had been tainted by negative media, especially in countries like Austria, Switzerland, Germany, Chile, and Argentina. Some of their perceptions were that black men are not intelligent, but dangerous and angry. Most of this information was what they gathered from old television shows that portrayed us in a less positive light. In my ten years abroad, I found myself constantly being an ambassador for black men. It was not on purpose, it just kept happening that way. There were always opportunities for me to be a negative or positive representation of the black man. And in those times, I chose the latter. Yes, when they initially saw me, they were intimidated (I am a 6' 8" black man—it comes with the shallow territory of appearance). But once they became acquainted with me and got to know me on a personal level, they would say, 'The things that I initially thought about you were wrong. You're nothing like I thought now that I have gotten to know you.'

"Once while living in Concepcion, Chile (South America), my wife befriended a young Chilean mother who lived near us. Her husband was the land overseer where a new building was being built. She lived on the property with her husband and young son in a temporary one-room shack. My wife and the young woman spent afternoons together trying to get to know each other using a Spanish/English dictionary for translations while her two-year old son played with our two- year old daughter. Weeks passed and we had not met her husband. My wife started to inquire about him to the young woman, telling her that he needed to meet me. So, one night late in the evening while we were already in bed, our doorbell rang. We did not answer it at first because we thought it was too late for anyone to be visiting. Then it rang multiple times afterwards, aggravating us to no end. I went to the door and looked through the peephole to see who was annoying us at such a late hour. When I looked through the magnifying hole, there was a short Chilean man who appeared disoriented and lost. I slightly opened the door and he commenced to doing a crazy dance right in front of me. He twisted himself around doing weird disco-type dance moves and then ended in the splits on the hall floor mumbling a few lyrics from the American singer James Brown's song 'Get on Up.' I thought that he was crazy. He had no doubt been drinking. It was all over his breath and I could smell it. All I could do was close the door and lock it. "Later we realized that he was the husband of my wife's new friend who did not speak any English. He was nervous about meeting a black professional basketball player. So, when he finally got the nerve to come over to our apartment after a few drinks, he literally embarrassed himself by demonstrating the only thing that he knew of African American men ... James Brown of all people, which is not an accurate representation of all black men.

"He eventually apologized to us days later (when he was sober) and we became good friends. But I did tell him not to ever do that again. My wife and I still laugh about that encounter. But it still stands true today. You cannot go around stereotyping individuals because of something you have only seen on television, or something that you have been conditioned to believe. You should not even do it because of something that you have heard. Trust me, you will embarrass yourself if you do. A wise man that I knew and respected once said, 'All wrong conduct is based on wrong thinking' (Dr. Edwin Louis Cole, father of the Men's Movement and author of *Maximized Manhood*).

"Although there were challenges and stereotypes that I had to overcome, being an ambassador for African American men was not intentional, but it was still an honor for me whenever the opportunity presented itself. By building relationships, I was able to break down many barriers of wrong thinking."

"After returning to the States, did you deal with the same issues?"

"Yes, I did. For some people it is easier to label you than to get to know you. But the thing they must be careful with is if they mislabel you, there is a chance that they will mishandle you. And if they mishandle you, brokenness is bound to take place. And what can you do with a broken man?

"God is a God of relationships. He designed us in His image. And if we are designed in His image, it is just wise to believe that we are to be people of relationships. You cannot say that you know a person unless you have a personal relationship with him or her. You cannot say that a man is your friend or your brother if you have never spent time with him and asked him about his story.

"I have experienced and witnessed unfavorable biases as an extremely tall black man. And that has been unfair on all levels. It is like a meter that gauges how much of a threat you are to other races. The meter reads like this: Yellow equals BE Careful he is a black man. Orange equals Keep Your Distance, he looks serious and talks with his hands. And Red equals High Alert, he is extremely tall (Lets create a narrative that poses him as a threat). Well, I cannot win for losing if this is the case. I am guilty on all three counts at no fault of my own. Threat stereotypes are one of the most inconveniently sad stereotypes ever allowed to grow and spread in this nation. Many black men, young and old, have lost their livelihoods and for some even their lives because of this deep-seated misperception. And you know what? That is a shame. And that shame belongs to a society that continues to water those seeds.

"Even being a black pastor in predominately white churches has its ups and downs as well. There are injustices all around. People just are not talking about it. You know how it is, they want everyone to believe that everything is kosher and that everyone means well towards each other. I have been in predominately white churches for over 25 years, and for a black man that is not an easy task. And if you think the scrutiny and the surveillance are not inside of those walls, then you are sadly mistaken. Diversity still comes at a price. There is just so much to learn. It does not just happen because a church decides that it wants diversity, it must be purposefully established and not something that is trumped up. It must be totally UNDIVIDED in all aspects and PURPOSEFULLY balanced.

"There needs to be conversations and cultural differences taught. This brings health into diversity. If you think that you have it all together and do not need training, that is an issue in and of itself. It does not just happen naturally. We do not get to pick and choose who has the conversation either. Everyone should be having the conversation. No one is exempt, least of all the church. It does not hurt to talk about it but try executing changes that will bring healing. That is when you know who is sincere about equality and diversity, and who is not.

"See, I know what it feels like to be a token and only allowed to preach on quote 'Black History Month' in predominantly white churches. I know what it feels like to have my words taken out of context and used against me. I know what it feels like to have other leaders misrepresent me and try to taint my character in a subtle way. I know what it feels like to have my leadership unjustly questioned after years of ministry. I know what it feels like NOT to have an advocate to fight for me in HR as a black man in the church. Now that is a pretty bad feeling. I know what it feels like to be misjudged because of implicit biases (unconscious biases). But even still I continue to put one foot in front of the other cultivating and harrowing over in the land where God has placed me. Not because it is a preference, but because it is a calling. There have been times when I wanted to give up and throw in the towel. Discouragement will do that to anyone. But with the help of God, I have always found a way to push through unnecessary boundaries. Do not get me wrong: NOT all my experiences in predominately white churches have been challenging. My family and I have benefited greatly, both physically and spiritually while being a part of churches that are still finding their places as multicultural congregations. I love and respect those that I had the privilege of serving alongside of. I have learned a lot in the last twenty-five years, and I continue to learn even more. And although there were challenges, I am the better for it. God has been in the center of it all and has always walked me through it.

"I do feel much better with where the church is heading right now in the years 2019 and 2020 as it relates to young black pastors getting the opportunities to excel as leaders in predominantly white megachurches. It has come a long way, and I know that it will get better. I do have to say that in my early days, the problem that I had in churches was that I was not a Dog & Pony Show. I just was not going to do that. I was not going to be a comedian on the platform or someone with a lot of flip and fluff. This is what some churches expect from black ministers (not to be too serious or to be over-the-top silly with an edge of entertainment). That is not me. I have also refused to sit on the sidelines as a 'Yes Man' (just being a representation of color without a voice). I have never been the perfect 'FIT' for some spaces created for me. But I do love the Lord and I do understand the calling on my life as a minister of the gospel. He did not create me to 'FIT' in. He created me to do His will and to minister the word to His people as He gives it to me.

"This is my concern when it comes to leadership diversity in the church. There must be an atmosphere where different styles are accepted and appreciated as important pieces of the body of Christ, especially if it is led by the spirit of God. This is what diversity is all about. This is what having a multicultural congregation is all about. When we value diversity, it enhances the identities of others. This is also true for predominately black churches that want to diversify. Again, no one is exempt. We all have a lot to learn. No church is perfect, but all should be striving to be as healthy as possible for the kingdom of God. If we are going to be the church, then let us be the church. And if we are going to love one another, then let us love each other and celebrate our diversities. 1 John 4:7–8 says, 'Beloved, let us love one another. For love is of God and everyone that loves is born of God and he that loves not, loves not God.' For God is love. And love qualifies you to say certain things. And so, it is in love that I am saying this so that the bride of Christ will be prepared for Him when He returns.

"Remember: When we say US and THEM, we stir the pot of division. Any race can be guilty of that."

"Have you ever been made to feel inferior to another race or culture?"

"I am sort of stubborn that way because my mother raised us not to look down on ourselves and not to allow the thoughts of others to dictate how we feel. We had to be people of faith and base our lives on the word of God. We have always refused to give anyone that kind of authority in our lives. I do not feel inferior to anyone, even if they tried to make me. I would not have been able to compete as a professional athlete if I did not have a sense of confidence in myself. That confidence has many times been misinterpreted as cocky and arrogant. But as I mentioned earlier, it is much easier to place a label on someone than it is to get to know them on a personal level. Whether playing professional basketball abroad or being in the U.S. marketplace and even in churches, I am always contending with a person's image of me. Their perception is as powerful as the truth because their perception can be their only truth, no matter how distorted it may be.

"It is funny how if you are a black man and you stand up for yourself or you carry yourself with dignity and assurance, it is interpreted as arrogant. As a believer in the Lord Jesus Christ, I understand that my confidence is in Him, and that statement is not a cliche.

"Once you read the word of God, it is the only book that as you read it, it is reading you. If I am going to be a man of faith, then that is what I will be. It takes faith to overcome certain things and that level of faith gives you the confidence that you need. God is serious about the faith factor. I would tell any young man, black or white, to base his life on the True

Foundation because anything else is faulty. If you are constantly building your life on the word of God and not anything that someone is interpreting to you, it will strengthen you. It is where I learned to gain my strength. To feel inferior to another race or culture would be like believing there is a supreme race and culture. And we all know this is not true. These matters that we deal with are 'Heart Matters' steeped in tradition, hatred, ignorance, and fear.

There is a threat that black men pose just by being born. Although it is not right, it is our reality." "My life Bible verse is Galatians 2:20, 'I have been crucified with Christ and I no longer live, but Christ lives in me. The life I now live in the body, I live by faith in the Son of God, who loved me and gave Himself for me' (NKJV)."

(According to the dictionary, the definition of *inferiority* is the condition of being lower in status or quality of others. To be degraded.)

"What would make you feel more valued and accepted as a black man in society today?"

"I already believe that I am a man of value and I have a lot to offer this world. My convictions do not allow me to sit around and wait to be accepted.

"Although society has evolved, there is still much work that needs to be done in terms of subtle systematic racism. I believe that a large part of the generation that carried that evil spirit of racism has died off and races are more empathetic towards one another. So, the challenges are not as great as they were before. I have many genuine friendships with people all over the world and the majority are of different races and cultures (particularly Caucasians). I feel very blessed to have these relationships. But it started because someone wanted to sincerely KNOW me, just as I did them. It took pursuing on both ends, laying down all preconceived notions and agendas, loving each other the way God intended us to love. I consider these men and women brothers and sisters in the Lord. We are like family and the trust level runs deep and spreads far. It is easy to trust someone when you know their true heart towards you. Even in that it takes faith. When you choose to love someone enough to journey alongside of them in this life, you welcome immeasurable possibilities for a unified society. My family and I believe wholeheartedly in diversity and multiculturalism. We hope that our lives are a good representation of unity with all people. The old saying, 'You can tell a tree by the fruit that it bears.' If you say you believe in diversity your lifestyle should show it.

"There cannot be any pretenses from either side when attempting to build relationships, or it eventually will be exposed and cause great detriment. Genuine friendships are important. If you say that we are friends or family even if we are of a different race, I will take you at your word and will expect to be treated as such. You should also expect the same from me.

"I know for some young black men, this can be difficult because when you are young, it is important to be accepted and to feel some sort of worth from others. Growing up in an environment that many black children grow up in, almost forces them to become great actors. Not hypocrites per say, but actors because they find themselves always adjusting their identities depending on where they are in society at the time. It is like being a chameleon. You must quickly learn to adjust and to be keenly aware of the environment you are in just to 'FIT' in at a moment's notice. You must give the impression that you are qualified to be there. All the while, the system believes that it is manipulating you to set the narrative. For me, growing up in an environment which was post-integration forced us to be that generation who were good at masking our feelings. To some degree there was this disguised frustration that we all possessed because we knew the struggle. Then there were some that did not know how to mask it well and they were the ones labeled as 'Troublemakers.' But those who were able to not only mask it but hide it could use it for the purpose of good. I think this was seen more in the athletic arena in basketball, football, and other sports because there was a platform by which frustration could be converted into energy and passion, then released in a positive way. Then you would be celebrated for it. That was the ironic thing about the athletes in my day. You could release those feelings on the court or field, but if you made some type of grimace or frown outside of the sports arena or spoke direct, you would be looked at differently. I am fifty-four years old and still today people misread my body language consistently. People are quick to tag you as being intimidating, angry, or intense. Again, this is not something I have heard, it is something that I have experienced through the years. If someone can label you, they think they have the upper hand on you. This is how they try to create the narrative for your life. Anytime you are mislabeled this can lead to being mishandled, undervalued, and mistreated. A lot of young black men and their families back in the day paid the price because of mislabeling in the system. Consequently, many labeled individuals were not able to get the same opportunities for educational advance-ments as their peers of another race. This would cause their families to suffer economically. The phrase 'WE HAVE TO BE TWICE AS GOOD AS THEY ARE' rings loud and true because as black men many of us recognize that the system's pen-dulum does not swing in the direction of mediocrity or just 'being good' when it comes to us. We must work so much harder and be so much better, if even to be somewhat noticed or given a fair chance."

(Although this phrase was not coined by a black man, it has been adopted and quoted by black people for years. But what has been left out was the other part written in an article by Harry Golden in 1963 where he quoted German/Jewish poet Heine, who was speaking to his fellow Jews after the ghet-to walls of Europe came down in the 19th century. Heine warned Jews before integrating into society, "We must be twice as good to get half as much." But further into the article Golden writes, "But for the Negro the odds are much higher. I believe that you must be five times as good to get one-half as much, and the only chance you have to reduce the odds, is education."

(This was written in an article by Harry Golden called "The American Negro and Higher Education in 1963." Published: *The Crisis*.)

I would like to see young black men excel in society without fighting a system that will initially stamp QUESTION MARKS upon their heads. That is no way to live. But if the battles must come, I pray that they would stand as strong as the genera-tions of old, being men that raise their families to be people of conviction, full of faith and fortitude, believing and valuing oneself even if no one else does.

> **"If you have no confidence in self, you are twice defeated in the race of life."** —Marcus Garvey

PART 4

CHAPTER 8

Millennial Memoirs

Times are changing and we are now entering the mind of a millennial who happens to be a young black man in his late twenties. Just how much life has he lived and to what depth of experience and knowledge has he gained growing up in an environment that has become quite different than that of his father, grandfather, and great-grandfather? There were sacrifices made so that he could walk towards the light that awaited generations before him. And although he is still miles from the end of the tunnel, he can see a glimmer of illumination that presents a ray of hope not only for his kind, but for all mankind. And for that, he is grateful. He does not boast of his upbringing, because he still does not comprehend the vast price that was paid. He just knows it was paid. He puts on "No Airs" because he is a young black man who was afforded some privileges that his great-grandfather does not even know exists. He embraces a pillow on his lap as he sits in front of a gas fireplace. He relaxes with a kind smile, waiting to answer questions that he has never been asked before. To a millennial, questions without any prep time could seem odd, but he took it all in stride and opened up the deepest parts of his heart. The tall burly guy is as gentle as they come. His expressions are sincere, and his peaceful disposition is an attention grabber which pulls on your heart strings. He is the type of man that you could be friends with forever. Maybe it is the loyalty within his eyes that gives it away.

What was going on in the mind of this young black man who wears his hair slightly shaven on the sides while the top of his head is crowned with kinky natural locks uncombed? One look at him and Madam C. J. Walker would wonder what all her efforts were for. Nonetheless, what did he know about being a pioneer in these times or tilling fallow ground for that matter?

What has he kept hidden in his short twenty-six years of life that no one has ever asked him about? What does this Urbanite have to convey to an audience of the unknown? How could he contribute to an interview of black men?

"How did you feel as a child in the 1990s and early 2000s being black? What differences did you notice?"

"As a young child I did not notice many differences between my life as a black person and the lives of my peers. I grew up just like everyone else. I was not socially or economically indifferent, and most of my childhood friends were of various races, particularly Caucasian. This was mainly because my parents raised us to appreciate other races and cultures. We spent a lot of time with other people cultivating relationships. It is the way my family still is today. We love diversity.

"I would not consider myself privileged, but my parents worked hard to take care of us. Our family lived in nice neighborhoods, attended some of the best schools in Texas, and went on summer vacations like most everyone else we knew.

"Growing up I never really dealt with the same type of racial biases or discrimination as some older people or older generations. But as I became older, I recognized and experienced subtle underlining tones of skepticism that led me to believe that there are certain biases against me.

"For instance, if I were involved in something at school and made a simple mistake or messed up, I was not given another chance. It would be totally blown out of proportion and they would be quick to give up on me and have a lack of confidence in me. But I noticed that my peers of another race would get those second and third chances, no matter what.

"Their mistakes were easily brushed off, all the while exclaiming that I was just going to be a troublesome kid, which was not true. Just seeing those patterns growing up made me think that I had to act a certain way or put on not necessarily a fake persona, but I had to act perfect all the time. There was this thought that I needed to dress a certain way, style my hair like everyone else and conduct myself in a way that would be acceptable to those around me. I soon found out that this was not getting me anywhere. I just wanted to be who God created me to be. As a young black man, I never wanted to be stereotyped, but most of the time it is inevitable. You cannot avoid it. I am twenty-six years old and I am more of a thinker than a talker. And with that, I have observed and experienced unfairness, whether it was intentional or not. I wished that adults over me when I was younger, whether in my school or in the workplace, would have understood that all I really wanted was a fair shot like anyone else. Not a handout, just fairness.

"In my years of playing sports in high school and college, I saw the political decisions made.

Unfortunately, even in my time spent in churches and on jobs in the marketplace, I have dealt with the frustrating emotions of others being chosen over me who did not have the credentials or experience that I have. But I am now seeing the world from different lenses. I can better understand some of the things that my dad has told me in the past about the reality of the world as it relates to black men." "What were the staple conversations of your time in your late teens and early twenties?"

"We discussed sports, school issues, music, things of the Bible, the latest athletic shoes, television celebrities, and what we wanted to do with our lives after college. We had a lot of big ideas and dreams. I can remember my first year of college hanging out with my roommate and a few other friends sitting around discussing the type of jobs that many black men were getting on television. We realized that some of them made it big because they were willing to put themselves out there dressed in drag (like women) to get funny reactions, particularly comedians. This opened up doors for them in the media and entertainment arena and they quickly became celebrity success stories. We had many deep conversations that veered in this direction because we were trying to figure out why this was accepted as a good thing. We understood the money factor, but how far does a black man need to go to become a celebrity?

"The fact that society has embraced black men as good entertainers can sometimes seem like there is not enough room to embrace us as intellects or men of greater substance. The entertainment business sometimes heavily suggested that black men do things that they were not always comfortable with just to get their feet in the door. I am sure it may have been like that back in the day when blacks had fewer opportunities of being on the big screen. But is it still happening today? It is like okay we are going to do something that you think is funny and get paid for it even though we know there may come a time when we are not taken seriously because of it.

"But those days should have come and gone. We as black men can do just about anything in the entertainment industry, or can we? We have choices, or do we?

"This entertainment situation is brimming because it has spilled over into churches as well. I have watched some black pastors and ministers on social media who literally are not as popular as white pastors if they share a serious, life-changing word. But if they are flamboyant and funny, almost in a comedic way, they become popular with the general public and most everyone wants to be associated with them. It is like society can accept us better if we live under that type of stigma. I do not think there is anything wrong with being funny, I just think this is another issue of stereotypical behavior that feeds more into how we are viewed, and this only leads to more racial biases.

"Am I grateful for black men of past generations? I am thankful for all who have paved the way and plowed diligently so that black men of today can have better opportunities, whether in the entertainment industries, athletic arenas, business world, or even in churches. It had to start somewhere. Someone had to be a pioneer, and pioneering is not always easy. Sometimes people did what they thought they had to do to make it, not realizing the consequences that may affect the future." (According to Wikipedia, Lincoln Theodore Monroe Andrew Perry, born in 1902, was believed to be the first successful black film actor. He was known in the 1930s for stirring up controversy and offense because of his character portraying a black man as a lazy, slow-witted coon. He acted on the white circuit with the stage name Stepin Fetchit ["The Laziest Man in the World"]. Although Mr. Perry was an intelligent man who was a writer for the premier African American newspaper *The Chicago Defender*, he still paid a costly price for the roles he played that were both stereo typically degrading and offensive towards the black population. He was never hired to play other roles outside of the Stepin Fetchit character. This is a prime example of not being able to move past a label that has been placed upon you.)

"Life is not important except in the impact it has on other lives." —Jackie Robinson

CHAPTER 9

Waiting for Change

"Are you content with the way society has treated black men as a whole?"

"No, because I feel like some people initially do not want to see our perspective. They do not think about how we feel and the things that we as black men deal with daily. There can be a lack of empathy on their part because they do not always see the underlying patterns of racism, so they cannot accept it as an issue. I wish that people would be willing to see our perspective so that we can have the CONVERSATION. We cannot have a dialogue, if only one party knows that something is not right, and the other party refuses to recognize it. I know that some Caucasian people are uncomfortable with having the conversation because of the shame of the past put on them through their ancestors, and so they choose not to talk about it. It is a reminder of what used to be so they would rather avoid the topic and act like nothing ever happened. But as a young person who wants restoration in our country, I believe it would be better to just air it out so that we can say this is what we had to go through and this is what we are dealing with now. We have struggles that many do not know about or even understand. If our voices are heard and what we say is deemed as an important priority, just maybe walls would begin to fall, and we would not have so much division.

"I do not think society fully understands the concept of our dealings with police officers, government officials, and systems in the workplace. All the things that black people have been trying to push through for years and years are taking a toll. It is tough to walk around with your guard up all the time because you just never know if you will be targeted in a racial hate crime or if there will be an issue of mistaken identity (that myth that we all look alike). These issues seem minimal to some, but for us, it is damaging. Each day a black man leaves his house, he is exemplifying bravery—physically, spiritually, and emotionally. If you are black, you get that. If you are not, think about it. It is like this constant glass ceiling that we can see our way out of but cannot quite break through. And it is either that we are not allowed to, or we are not set up for success in a way to do so.

"If we were offered more tools for success or if someone was just eager to say, 'Here's how I can help you, or I do not have extra resources, but I hear what you are saying, and I want to try and understand,' I think that would help us work through it and maybe help us change our perspectives towards one another. My life Bible verse is Joshua 1:9 which says, 'Have I not commanded you? Be strong and of Good courage; do not be afraid, nor be dismayed, for the Lord your God is with you wherever you go' (NIV)."

As he shared his thoughts, I could see the disparity in his eyes. He desired change like it was a distant antidote to a deadly disease. Although it seemed far away, he still held on to hope because he knows that things could be better, he just did not comprehend why it was easier said than done.

He experienced the good life as a child, hardly noticing the cruel and unfair world that he lived in. A life surrounded by family and friends in Suburbia USA filled with barbecues, community events, and neighborhood diversity—that was all he knew. But as the years passed, he could see that things were more complicated than he'd ever imagined. He was no longer the cute little black kid on the block; he became the young strong black man growing up in a society that was not always kind to those who looked like him. Parents constantly preaching to him to be careful of profiling, "You may be targeted," and praying for him each time he walked out of the house. Nonetheless, he has always remained optimistic and has not given up on people. He has a heart for all people and the promise of unity. He acquired the right not to be content with the way society has treated black men. I am sure this was passed down to him by the men in his family. He chooses not to use it as a weapon or excuse, only as a longing and stirring for change. There have been numerous discussions among young black men and older black men concerning the challenges of the day. What works and what has not worked. Everyone is looking for direction and waiting for a transformation. When will the process begin? The fact of the matter is that the transformation process began 155 years ago. It is just taking a lot longer than expected.

"Have you ever been made to feel inferior to another race or culture?"

"Well ... not really. I guess I grew up in a time that people were more aware and 'tried' to be better about what they said and did. So, I do not think that I have ever been in a situation where it was blatant. I mean, there have been times that people have said derogatory things to me that implied that was happening, but I'm sure it was nothing compared to things that may have been said to my dad or grandfather back in the day to make them feel inferior. I think in my case as a young black man, I have been subtly reminded to be sure to stay in my own lane. I am not oblivious to that. Because I am a former college basketball player, that lane has been designated for me. In other words, they cannot see the value of what else I bring to the table simply because they have placed me in a box of just the one talent that I possess. They find it difficult to move past it. Like I alluded to before, if we as black men are not bringing something along the lines of entertainment, it is much harder for us to be popular in society. I am not overlooking the fact that my talent has opened doors of opportunities for me, I just do not want one talent to rule out all the others because of limited mindsets.

"As it relates to culture, because of my mom and dad I have been exposed to so many different cultures.

Although both of my parents are African American, I was born abroad in South America in Rio Claro, Brazil. And because of this I have a dual citizenship (American/Brazilian). I grew up in America with Indian friends, black friends, Hispanic friends, and white friends. Even my sister kept a diversity of friends. That was normal life for us. At a young age, I knew that God wanted me to be a part of bridging the gap between races. It was no surprise when I became older, I met and fell in love with someone of a different race. My wife is a white German/Canadian woman. And although her race had nothing to do with the reason that I married her (I married her because I love her), I do believe that it played into what God put in my heart years ago.

"When you marry someone of a different race and culture it is a privilege because you get to learn so much about who they are and why they do things a certain way, or differently than you. You begin to understand and appreciate those differences, figuring out ways to blend it all together. I wanted to mirror the love that God has for all people and be an example of unity. Being married teaches you how to love unconditionally because you are going to be with that person for the rest of your life."

"Has it been difficult being married to someone of a different race?"

"Well, it has a few challenges. Not in how we feel towards one another, but how we are viewed by others when they see us together because we are a biracial couple. There have been black women who give us 'THE LOOK' at times when we are out together. They have facial expressions that simply ask, 'What are they doing together?' As though we are not supposed to be together. And I am sure that it happens the same for my wife as well when white guys see us together. But we have gotten used to it. This is our story and we are confident in who we are as a couple. When God is in the center of a relationship, He will show Himself faithful and make all things well. If God is in the center of our relational society, He will show Himself faithful and make all things well.

"See, ultimately it really does not matter what people think, because for me I have never cared whether a person is white, black, Hispanic, Asian, or whatever; people are people and love is love. I just hope that our relationship will inspire others to think the same. And if anything, lead them to begin having those tough conversations about race and unity."

"What would make you feel more valued and accepted in society today?"

"I would like for other races to understand where I am, who I am, and the fact that I am a young person with hopes of a bright future. I am not one-dimensional. Yes, I am a black man and yes, I am tall, but this does not make up who I am entirely. It would be nice if people could see past the outward appearance and look a little deeper. Looking at the outward appearances only creates more stereotypical ideas. I studied theology in college for five years. I love to cook and have deep discussions. I am computer savvy and proficient with technology. I love music and lots of other things. But I think it is hard for some people to see that because they are blinded by what they really want to see, and that is not right. "I think that most young black men just want to be accepted and valued as MEN, period. Many of us want to be acknowledged as decent human beings with good heads on our shoulders without being stereotyped or the worst being expected of us. We want to feel supported and encouraged by our society. You know, like the world that we live in has our backs and has our best interests at heart. The American press clearly shows that the black man's best interest is not taken to heart. Breaking news of black men being killed on the regular (by bad law enforcement) like it is a sport or hobby. When this happens, every man in America should stand up and demand change in the system before it is too late. Everyone is crying out that enough is enough, but things only seem to be getting worse. When it affects one of us, it affects us all. We all at one time or another have stopped in our tracks and said, 'That could have been me.' And that can be very disheartening.

"It would also be nice to be followed down different avenues where we offer a numerous amount of creative abilities, visions, dreams, and new ideas. We would love to have intellectual conversations with the best of them, being received as professional in our own way (a suit and tie does not always count), even if we do not have celebrity status, money, or political influence. To initially be judged by the shade of our skin puts us in a grave situation because there are many of us, but we are not the same. Skin color is superficial and has no bearing on a person's integrity, or lack of. We are each motivated by the character instilled in us. But of course, we live in a time when everyone should know this. We are a diverse group of people inside a diverse group of people. God intended it to be this way. There is much to learn about each of us and much to be appreciated. With proper training and getting to know one another personally, we should be able to work through unconscious biases as a human race."

"Diversity is not about how we differ. Diversity is about embracing another's uniqueness." —Ola Joseph

The young man expressed the beauty of love and its inspiration. If we understood what love is and what it does, there would be the possibility of living in harmony with all men, no matter who they are and where they come from. God's love does amazing things when we live by its attributes. Our prayer as a nation should be that we are motivated by the true love of God for our fellow men. God's love draws and unites. It stabilizes shaky ground and secures our foundation. It breaks down walls and removes chains. It rebukes wrong and seeks good in everything. It speaks kindness and is considerate in all times. It empathizes and its peace is contagious in the most absolute way. God's love dispels fear and builds trust. There is nothing that it cannot heal or forgive. It patiently waits and does not push ahead. God's love will protect and fight for the least of them. And when we fail, His love will remain unfailing. The young man believes this with all his heart.

Author's Conclusion

My four-day interview concluded with four men who have never asked anything of society. They have only expected what is due and fair. And who is to say what is due and fair, if anything. What measures can be projected in this instance? Yes, it is true everyone wants something out of this world. It is human nature in wishing to be catapulted into a personal destiny by using every means to get there. No one is exempt from this, and every man is counted in his own right as an eligible recipient of a promising destiny. What better place to be counted than in the United States of America? This is the place that prides itself on being the land of the free and the home of the brave. It owns up to the words of its constitution and strongly defends the rights of all men—so it is believed. But there has been a bigotry in our nation that has suppressed and stifled the growth of its character. And without growth, deterioration takes place, and eventually death. There must be this idea of harvesting, striving to foster life. This is how we flourish and build the character of a nation, remembering our stance of moral uprightness that "All Men are created equal ..."

African American men have come a long way in this land, from the heated cotton plantations of the south, the farms and cornfields of the Midwest, and the crowded walls of industrial factories in the north. After many years of slavery and being downtrodden under the banners of segregation, discrimination, and inequalities, black men have become some of the most elite figures in our nation with accolades reigning in sports, entertainment, business, politics, inventions, military rankings, and many other top-tier professions. They have contributed considerably to the land of opportunity. An applause is due their service for what most said could not be done. But then there are the unknown pioneers with invisible merits under their names that few will ever see or even know existed. I began these series of interviews with a 96-year-old former sharecropper who knew the value of hard work and what it took to prepare for a grand harvest. It was a prized inheritance that was passed down from his father and grandfather—priceless gems that could only be given as a rich legacy and nothing more. He did not waste his time worrying about the obstacles that stood in his way or the conditions of his environment. He just did the best that he could do with what he had, and he kept moving forward with determination. How many people would know the years of gritting his teeth and saying nothing because he was addressed as "BOY" even at the ages of 30 and 40? Who would know about his lonely times in the dried fields of the hot sweltering countryside picking cotton with callused hands that sometimes bled at night? Who cared to know that he pushed through against all resistance, sometimes pulling the plow and other times driving the plow? Either way, the plowing had to be done and he was the one to do it. His lot in life was not made to be easy, but it was the only way the process of growth could take place. And so, he proceeded with vigor and steadfastness.

You see, what some people do not understand is that in order to experience a harvest, it takes an enormous amount of determination and patience through some days of pain and maybe some nights of suffering. There must be courage, knowing when to speak and when to remain silent in the circumstances of the land. Farmers are faith-filled individuals who operate that way. They strategically put in the work based on the season and then trust that the harvest will come. You never give up if you desire the rewards of a bumper crop. First rule of thumb: focus straight ahead, regardless of the unforeseen elements that are sure to creep up in efforts to destroy what you have started. Diligence is the thorough keeping of what is sacred in the value of sowing and reaping a rich legacy. All the hard work put in and waiting for the fruit of that harvest is part of the ongoing process. And that process is not in vain.

And although the sharecropper found it difficult at times to turn soil on fallow ground, he could rest assured that there are many unknown pioneers following in his footsteps that would continue to till the ground, plow its foundation, and plant seeds of life for the benefit of a harvest in this country.

Black men should be proud of their heritage and where they come from. No one should be allowed to tell them otherwise. They have earned the rights to all words printed in the Declaration of Independence: "Life, Liberty, and the Pursuit of Happiness ..."

I believe the four generations of men would like their words to transform situations, prick hearts, and soothe souls, bringing forth an awareness of historical patterns that continue to manifest themselves in our present day. Being politically correct is irrelevant at this point. Their intentions were noble and never to inadvertently offend. Can a black man really be diplomatic in his own defense?

I asked only that these men be candid, and with that there was no sugarcoating to make their words palatable. There is a fearless truth that hangs in the balance of being both forthright and sincere. I dared not hold them in contempt because of their vulnerability. I searched for a raw and organic dialogue and that is exactly what I received. Perhaps their statements are true for some African American men, and for others not so much. Everyone's story is different. And maybe the melting pot of America is a blend of individuals who are coexisting under unrealistic terms.

Whatever the case may be, we as a human race must find some common ground of mutual respect and a love for life in general. We cannot argue with respect because it will deliver justice. And we cannot argue with love because it will cast down all fears. Where there is no fear, threat is diminished, and we move forward in unity. Our souls must remain well in all things, despite unfortunate circumstances that leave us feeling frustrated, especially if we trust that GOOD will ultimately triumph over evil. We see the crude calamity of our nation with naked eyes that sting at the sight of it.

These unfiltered memoirs of ordinary black men were written to the American Public to alter the course of catastrophe in our society. What I gathered is that true unadulterated repentance must take place and heartfelt forgiveness needs to be generously poured out if our nation is to do more than survive. The ashes and debris of slavery, lynching, Black Codes, Jim Crow laws, redlining, injustice, and inequality still fogs the atmosphere like the aftermath of a smoldering building that has burned for days. And unless there is a purging, the dust will never settle and be swept away. Its residue will continue to reside in almost every place, and the cycle will persist in choking our nation. What many believe to be a white versus black crisis has kept us divided and unsettled. But the real issue lies in the hearts of those who do not know love.

We are not dealing with a race matter, but rather Matters of the Heart that some have not relinquished to Jesus. And because of this they are deceived, and their actions cause affliction and anguish on others. This country needs a healing that only God can give. And if we ask, He will be faithful to do it. We must place our land back under the mighty hand of God if we are to be bountiful in the harvest. There is much work to be done and we cannot succeed without the unity of all. The process is laborious, but the outcome will be profitable to the soul. What if America understood the process of plowing from generation to generation? Would empathy arise?

The challenges of plowing are what made the old sharecropper stronger and more resilient. He handled the pressures of the land with grace and dignity, choosing not to be defeated physically or mentally. And in the end, he is victorious just as he believes those following in his footsteps will be. The day of reckoning has come to the land, and now is the time for all to reap its harvest.

I implore you to receive what you will and find a way to not only understand the black man's perspective but be compelled to walk out God's original plan for true diversity in America, one that includes justice, impartiality, and being equally esteemed. This is a gift to all MEN. And who has the authority to deny them of a gift given to them by God and established in our constitution? And so, they continue to press onward believing that one day society will do right by every individual who considers America HOME. Many seasons have come and gone in the last 400 years, and the transformation of a society is still in progress. For black men in America it is not "We Shall Overcome Someday," it is "We Are Overcoming Each Day" one plow at a time.

The End

CPSIA information can be obtained
at www.ICGtesting.com
Printed in the USA
FSHW010809021120

9 781977 229960